In Praise of *Nurtured by Nature, Book I*

"Your book, *Nurtured by Nature,* I enjoyed reading it! I could visualize the landscape, the homes, and the people who lived in them – it was like being back in Abercrombie, [North Dakota]. Your book gave me such joy to read ...." – Annette E.

"You are fantastic at writing and making us feel like we are right along with you. Such a joy!" – Bernie R.

"I've read your book. It is fascinating to hear [read] what life was like growing up on the farm in Minnesota." – Diane J.

"I'm so grateful for the inspiration you are to all of us. Indeed, all of us are worth a book of stories as we share a bit of life-wisdom and God's wisdom through our stories." – Father Duane P.

"Your story is yet another testament of God's plan for you. Your book is a treasure." – Carolyn T. B.

"Alice Gunness' combination of personal experience, faith, humor, and trust in God brings new and practical meaning to the wisdom of the Beatitudes. Her book is a well of spiritual strength and nourishment and is certain to be a comfort to all who read it." – Eunice H.

Nurtured by Nature

BOOK II

A RICH HERITAGE TO CHERISH

To Nikki

Enjoy!

Alice Bjorklund Gunness

Alice B Gunness

WESTBOW
PRESS®
A DIVISION OF THOMAS NELSON
& ZONDERVAN

WestBow Press books may be ordered through booksellers or by contacting:

WestBow Press
A Division of Thomas Nelson & Zondervan
1663 Liberty Drive
Bloomington, IN 47403
www.westbowpress.com
844-714-3454

Cover photo of Alice holding her first book courtesy of Dave Samson and The Fargo Forum.

ISBN: 978-1-6642-0875-9 (sc)
ISBN: 978-1-6642-0874-2 (hc)
ISBN: 978-1-6642-0876-6 (e)

Library of Congress Control Number: 2018906077

Print information available on the last page.

WestBow Press rev. date: 11/03/2020

Contents

Dedication

To my family

Preface

Nurtured by Nature: Book II follows Alice Gunness' well-received first book *Nurtured by Nature* (2018, WestBow Press). I welcome you to continued memoir stories and essays from the Red River Valley of the North. The stories tell of Alice's childhood, her husband Donald's growing up years, and stories passed down by the generation before them. We learn of Alice and Donald's family on their farm near Abercrombie, North Dakota.

Nature, family, faith, and one generation preparing for the next to live more comfortable lives of purpose are among the topics in Alice's stories. She focuses our vision for a close look at nature. For example, describing wildflowers she spots as a young girl bringing cows home from pasture, and referring to autumn birch leaves as golden coins. Broad universal themes and topics reveal themselves as Alice considers joys and hardships in the lives of immigrants who left Scandinavia for America – the new country. We learn of her father, John Bjorklund's, winters as a logger in the Minnesota Northwoods, working to save money for a farm. Alice gives readers stories of Donald's parents and the early business community they helped establish. Her faith shines in stories of daily life and reflections on God's grace and mercy. Bible verses, or the lyrics of old familiar hymns, complement her memories. We also learn of her life's absurdities, including giggling in church and running from a rooster.

Alice Gunness and I met four years ago when the Riverview Writing Crew formed as a writing seminar at Riverview Place, in Fargo, North Dakota. Our group consists of Riverview residents, and writers from the Fargo-Moorhead area; at times supported by grants from Humanities North Dakota. Group members often were the first readers of Alice's writings. Our core of eight writers, and the additional ten attending when possible, congratulate Alice! It is a pleasure to co-lead the group with Rita Greff and David Morstad.

Alice is a memoirist. Readers might easily find a friendship with Alice through her voice in these heartfelt stories. Her youngest son told me, "I think Mom's found her passion as a writer."

Karla Smart-Morstad, Ph.D.
Professor Emerita
Concordia College
Moorhead, MN
Soli Deo Gloria

Introduction

The second book of *Nurtured by Nature* is a continuation of our family stories. I also tell about our ancestors and what they experienced. My husband's family came to America in 1882, with Donald as a member of the fourth generation of the Gunness family in the new country. I am a member of the first generation of a Swedish family who came over to America in the early 1900s.

Donald Gunness and I raised five children on our farm near Abercrombie, North Dakota. These stories are written for our grandchildren, to share with them when difficulties may come, so they may be over-comers as was their family before them, with God's help.

I include stories of my own childhood telling of our immigrant family from Sweden headed by my parents John and Ottilia Bjorklund. Their stories start with John's logging camp experiences. Money from logging helped them buy a farm which they did as newlyweds in 1917.

Donald's parents, Arthur and Adelia Gunness, married in the mid-1920s, shared a life probably not at all as they expected. Art and Dilly were both born in the centennial year of 1900. With God's help they survived and were resilient through adversity. Together they endured the 1929 Stock Market Crash, the Great Depression and drought years of the 1930s, and World War II during the 1940s. Art was a Richland County Commissioner and Dilly played the church organ for thirty years. Donald's parents died early. His father of a heart attack at age fifty-eight and his mother at age sixty after a cancer battle.

I include multi-generational stories of love and laughter, difficulties and challenges, but most of all survival during the years that brought the Stock Market Crash in 1929, the Great Depression, the Second World War, and the Dust Bowl drought of the 1930s.

My husband's Uncle Syvert wrote these words:

> *The heritage is that we come from proud, industrious and still humble people. Proud in that it was well-recognized, that one should take pride in everything attempted, one should always do his best no matter the task. Industrious in that they knew the world did not owe them a living and that any accomplishment had to be earned. Humble in that everything they had was considered a blessing from God and they believed that Jesus was their Savior. Ours is a choice to perpetuate or let this rich heritage diminish.*

Chapter One

Childhood Memories

Part One **Early Memories**

Playing Chicken

I t seemed like each spring when my mother ordered baby chicks – always Leghorns – delivered to the post office, they were all very hungry and very noisy! All 100 of them. Among the chicks there were about five to ten roosters, and among those that did not turn into spring fryers there would be an occasional mean rooster as they grew. I cannot remember how we knew they were different, but they seemed ornery and worried the hens.

Well, there was only one way to handle that. The rooster needed to be teased and provoked to see what would happen next. So, at age five, what else could a bored child do? Following my older brother's example, I would go up to an ornery rooster stomping my feet, just so far, three or four steps, and the rooster would turn around with feathers fluffed and a mean gleam in his eye. He came charging after me, but only three or four feet at a time. I would return the favor, and go after him, only three or four feet at a time. He would retreat, never turning around, but getting a little more riled each time.

For a bored five-year-old, this was great fun! This back and forth movement continued for about fifteen minutes or so until all of a sudden, the rooster did not stop at three or four feet. Instead, he kept on coming! After me! Then I was in trouble. If a rooster caught you, they would jump up and scratch your bare legs and feet with their talons and claws. I headed for the house, but the rooster was too close behind me! Too close indeed! I knew I could not stop to open the screen door or he would get me. I yelled to my mother to open the door, after I had run around the house to gain speed, hopefully getting ahead of him so I could dash in the front door. My mother was always faithful. (I did it more than once). It was usually before noon dinner so I knew she would be in the kitchen. There she stood in the open doorway waiting for me. Talk about crazy, dumb things to do. But oh, IT WAS FUN!

Under the Railroad Train

The main line train track ran past our farm, just beyond our front yard, when I was growing up. There was also a switching track alongside, so trains would sometimes stop and wait for another train on the sidetrack. They would meet each other going opposite directions.

The train track served as our private path walking to and from school every day. Sometimes there would be a long freight barreling through. The engineer would open his window and wave, and I would wave back, standing on the outside edge of the sidetrack. I am sure my mother was watching for me with the coffee pot on after school.

Once when I was about seven-years old, there were free movies in our little town about a half mile away. Of course, I fell asleep – my bedtime was 8 p.m. After the movie was over, we walked home. All except this dear girl because my father could not wake me up! So, he lifted me up and carried me home in his arms until we came to the railroad crossing over the driveway to our farm. A big, long freight train sat over our driveway, waiting to meet another train. My dad woke me up and said, "We have to crawl under the boxcar together." But I was scared. I protested, "The train might start up when we are under and we might be run over, let's crawl up the ladder to the top and go down the other side." "No," he said, "that would not work."

We stood hashing over what we were going to do. The endless patience of my dad! He encouraged me that we could do it – go under the train car. Finally, I realized I had no choice. We crawled under the boxcar and came out on the other side of the train. The train did not move! Surprise! We were home at last.

Bringing Home the Cows

S ummer is never long enough in our north country. We grab on to
lovely spring days and hold them close, knowing they won't come
every day, one after the other. So, it is with great joy that we rejoice
over the arrival of warm summer days.

One of my jobs during childhood summers was to bring the
cows home from the pasture for evening milking time. I'd walk the
long lane, hedged by row upon row of fence posts and barbed wire
to protect the field crops beyond. It was fun to watch them grow.
When I came to a rise overlooking the swamp, I'd call out, "Come
Boss! Come Boss!" Some cows were lying down, resting and chewing
their cuds. They heard my call and raised their heads, then got up
and began to walk for home. The lead cow was always in the front
and all the other cows acknowledged her.

In the spring, Tamarac trees in the small copse were regaining
their needles. It is the only evergreen tree that sheds its needles each
fall. The smell of fresh evergreens could only be surpassed by the
soft, velvety feel of the needles. I stroked the limbs, so soothing to
the touch. Then I took notice of the miniature blooms fastened to the
branches. They resembled tiny, red roses. They nestled in the limbs
and, oh, they were so beautiful. On the ground, wild strawberries
were hiding. Not so many, just a few to enjoy on the way. They were
small and red, and so sweet. Another surprise!

In early June, gorgeous, big clumps of Marsh Marigolds were in
full bloom at the edge of the swamp. They like their feet to be a little
damp. One time in June I spied a Lady Slipper or Moccasin Flower

of delicate pink and white growing by the edge of the creek. I didn't pick it because it is Minnesota's State Flower and they are protected.

One August, I found a wild Tiger Lily blooming in the swamp. How did it get there? As the days shortened, the Maple trees in the lane began to lighten and change to brilliant shades of red and orange.

My Swedish mother told about spending her childhood summers up on the *saeter*, or mountain, living in huts with her older sister. They herded the cows, milked every day, and made cheese. Family would come weekly to check on them, deliver food and take the cheese back.

She spoke lovingly of her experiences, as I do, too. It was no chore bringing the cows home each evening. I learned from nature every day, even watching the wood chuck amble across the lane to his home in the rock pile.

Taking the Cows to Pasture

One year my dad purchased an eighty-acre tract of land adjoining our property. It was all woodland and was across the railroad tracks from our farmstead. The first several winters were spent cutting down the trees for firewood. Then, after the roots had rotted for several years, he dynamited the stumps out of the ground during the summer. As a child, I worried about dynamite. I listened for the loud bang and then wondered if my dad got out of the way in time. My mother saw that I was worried. She told me my dad knew how to handle dynamite and not to worry, but I still worried.

One summer, as we entered the month of August, the pastures were very short of moisture. My dad decided to put the cows on the grass coming nicely after the stump removal. It would involve taking the cows across the railroad tracks after the evening milking. As we were finishing chores, my dad asked me to run down the driveway to check the railroad tracks to see if there were any trains coming. "Look both ways for trains and come back and tell me if you can see any coming," he said. There was a long freight train that barreled through, at 7:00 p.m. each evening, coming from the northwest on its main route from Winnipeg, Canada to the Twin Cities of Minnesota. The train came through about the same time we finished milking. Dad wanted to be very sure that we missed that one.

We could see the train tracks for a mile or more before they turned out of sight, so we could take the cows across the tracks if there was no train coming. My brother and I each had an assignment. Mine was to stand by the open gate to the pasture and my older brother was to stand on the driveway to keep the cows from going on the road to town. What responsibilities! It was very scary for me. The cows were as nervous as I was. As they approached the railroad track, they started to run. They knew the train came through at that time as well as we did.

With their bags empty of milk, it was quite a sight to see them running, with their udders swaying back and forth in front of their hind legs. As soon as they were across the tracks, they walked the rest of the way—about a city block—to where I was standing. Into the pasture they went, and we all breathed easier.

These memories remain fresh with me to this day. Did someone say living on a farm was dull?

Fruiting Our Way Out West

There were four of us, two sisters, another friend from our community, and me. I was invited to travel with them to the western states. We were going to help harvest fruit along the way to pay for our trip. What an adventure! It was 1952 and I was eighteen!

We began our trip one beautiful June morning. It was a lovely, sunny day to travel and enjoy the changing scenery. I was surprised to find cattle grazing in open country with no fences in western North Dakota. We had to stop several times as the cattle were crossing the highway in front of us.

Our first experience was picking cherries off the trees in Washington state. We climbed ladders to reach the cherries and filled our sacks with them. They were on the sour side, not good for eating. They were headed for a canning factory.

In Oregon, with a beautiful view of Mount Hood, we crawled on our hands and knees, picking luscious red strawberries. We ate as we picked. We stayed there for two weeks and on the Fourth of July drove up Mount Hood and watched the skiers above the snowline. We had saved enough money to enjoy a wonderful meal on top of the mountain.

Leaving Oregon, we headed to California hoping to pick peaches. We were turned down as we were only girls and we would not be able to carry the sacks on our shoulders. They did not know about us girls from Minnesota carrying heavy milk pails. He directed us to a local canning factory, where we applied, but only night work was available. We had to make enough money to return home, so we took the jobs.

They set us on stools in front of a conveyor belt that carried the peaches. On the conveyor stood knives that we were supposed to slam our peaches on. The peaches were the hard, clingstone variety. Working as fast as possible, we had to place the peaches in the right positions on the knives so they could be sliced in half. It was hard, boring work, working nights and sleeping days. Maybe! We rented a cheap place to stay and we made enough money to return home.

Our one big stop on the way home was through Colorado Springs to see Pike's Peak. But, it was covered with clouds. We drove on to Denver and went downtown to do some shopping. I bought a beautiful wool suit, with a slim skirt and a boxy jacket. I felt very chic, and that suit carried me through three more years of college and teaching. We drove through the golden wheat fields of Kansas at harvest time and then turned north on Highway 81.

We returned safely home with no problems, but I think we were very tired of each other's company. We were all just glad to get home. It was quite an experience at my age, working our way through the western half of the country, but I am not sure I would recommend it for someone today.

Minnesota 4H Clubs

I pledge my head to clearer thinking,
My heart to greater loyalty,
My hands to larger service,
And my health to better living,
For my home, my club, my community, and my country.

This pledge was recited at the beginning of every monthly 4H meeting. 4H Clubs were wonderful community events, supplying many of our social needs ages ten to eighteen. At the meeting of our club, with about twenty kids, our leader was an older woman who had taught school in her younger days. Her daughter played the piano, and everyone joined in singing from the 4H Songbook, including our parents. Meetings were carefully planned with a songfest to begin the evening. Songs like "The Church in the Wildwood" and "Can She Bake a Cherry Pie, Billy Boy" rang out at each meeting.

A business meeting followed, with duly elected officers each year following *Robert's Rules of Order.* A program was next. Different members put on a program each month with help from their parents. It was interesting and fun.

Sometimes there were demonstrations in preparation for the County Fair. One of my most embarrassing moments occurred when my leader, Mrs. Sundberg, convinced me to give a demonstration about brushing my teeth. There I stood, spitting the toothpaste and saliva into a basin before me. Then taking water rinsing my mouth and spitting again. I wanted to die. It was my last demonstration. We all had to complete a health project, and a gardening one as well.

An incident occurred when I was in a meeting held at someone's home. I was just old enough to attend. It happened that the dining room floor was badly slanting. We paid no attention until, during the business meeting, the sewing machine suddenly rolled across the floor. We all started giggling. It was the highlight of the evening!

We looked forward to the East Ottertail County Fair each year held in Perham, Minnesota, the last days of July. Everyone displayed their vegetables in a box and competed for first prize. I think we had to have six different vegetables to qualify. The girls sewed dresses they entered, after taking Home Economics in high school, and the boys brought cornstalks, small grains, and animals for their projects. We had a big, beautiful 4H Building on the fairgrounds. In addition to individual projects, each club was given a four-by-eight display booth to creatively promote their 4H club. The clubs competed against each other. Ribbons were given in each category.

Each Grand Champion ribbon winner was given a trip to the State Fair held at the end of August before school started. There were activities planned for all year – a spring One Act play, a summer garden tour to each member's home, a basket social, and preparing for the County Fair before winning a trip to the Minnesota State Fair. We rode the train to the State Fair and were dropped off at the 4H building. There were bunk beds, three high, all over the huge dorm room. Now we were on our own. It was a delightful learning experience that gave us courage for high school and college.

4H Clubs gave us a wonderful opportunity to grow and mature, to accept responsibility, and to work together with others. We were learning life's lessons in a meaningful way. It was worth it!

Thank you 4H Clubs.

Lake Marion Swimming –
How I learned to Swim

E very summer afternoon, if it was warm and sunny, we would go swimming. (As memory has it, that was every day in my childhood!) Since I was the youngest, about six-years old, I was duly instructed by my siblings that I must stay close to shore because I did not know how to swim yet. The older kids proceeded to enter deeper water to the diving board.

They were always having such a good time with their friends laughing, shouting, and showing off a bit. I could clearly hear them by the shore, and I was lonesome. I made up my mind that I was going to join their fun. So I walked into the ever-increasing depths of water, despite the kids yelling, "Go back, Alice, go back."

All of a sudden, I entered deeper water and my feet went out from under me. I started to swim the dog paddle. I could really swim! They stood looking at me as I came closer. There were no congratulations, just sink or swim. After that I was not afraid of the water anymore.

Swimming Lessons

Beginning in the 1940s, in Ottertail County, Minnesota, the Red Cross gave weekly swimming lessons at area lakes. Lake Marion was one of the sites. I think everyone started at the same level, whether older or younger. We had an hour or two class each week with a college-aged male instructor whom we adored.

We would start out on land practicing our strokes. Starting on one foot, we would coordinate arms and leg movements, learning how to breathe with each stroke as well. Soon we were able to stand in shallow water, practicing again until we had our strokes learned. Then we would go to deeper water to practice the swimming procedure. Soon we were swimming, in varying degrees, with our instructor carefully monitoring until we all got it right.

The swimming lessons lasted six to eight weeks all summer each year. Class went from beginners to intermediate, to advanced, and then to learning to dive into the water. After that came junior and senior lifesaving classes. There were six years of lessons by the time we finished. We all were pretty good swimmers.

We had to prove we had accomplished each goal by learning the different strokes and improving on them. Then we were tested to make sure we were qualified for the next year's session. We also needed to practice lifesaving techniques, in case we ever needed them, by learning holds to bring our victims to shore.

I am so thankful for such a wonderful program provided for us. I made sure our children all learned to swim by taking lessons in a neighboring town's pool.

Fourth of July

Each summer, Don and I and our family were invited to a cousin's lake cabin for the Fourth of July. The kids could not wait to get in the water. Sometimes a brisk northwest wind blew across the lake on the Fourth. Don's elderly cousin would sit in his lawn chair, overlooking the water, with his winter parka on! Sometimes the water was warmer than the air.

The water was quite deep and rocky by the dock. Our children were younger than Don's brother's family, so I stayed on the dock in case help was needed. Suddenly I realized that my nephew, Steve, about eight-years old, was struggling in the water beside me. I watched him sink under the water and come up again. I realized he could be in trouble. I quickly grabbed him out of the water and hauled him onto the dock. He had lost hold of the dock and slipped on a rock underneath of it.

He sputtered angrily as he came out, "I almost drowned in that dirty water!" I was so glad I was there. Since then, going swimming has never been his favorite sport.

The Rip Trip

There were four of us. Frances, a little older gal, Jim a fellow high schooler as was I, and my older brother Clarence. We each liked a certain person in our group, but it was not returned. I liked Jim, but Jim liked Frances, Frances liked Clarence. I do not know who Clarence liked. Oh! The unrequited love of a fifteen year old.

When we were younger, we skied down a small hill on the farm where we lived. We also had a sturdy sled my dad made. But we were older now and needed a new challenge. Jim suggested that we ski south of town in a hilly area, about two miles away. We all agreed. We came to a large hill facing the lake. The hill was very high and a long way down. The wind had blown off most of the snow on the hillside with only short grass to hold any snow.

We talked about trying it, as we lay in the warm sun on the hillside. Clarence only had clamp skis. The rest of us had straps to hold our feet in place. We asked each other, "How would we stop? What if we fell"? My mother was always sure one of us would break a leg!

Finally, I suggested, "How about sitting down on our skis"? They all hooted at my idea, but I decided to try it. I sat down on my skis and slowly proceeded down the hill. As I started to pick up speed, suddenly a sharp-edged rock appeared protruding out of the ground before me. I was headed right for it. I called to the others, "There's a sharp rock ahead." They laughed even louder.

As soon as I saw it, I made my skis straddle the rock. As I went over it, right between my legs, I felt and heard a ripping sound coming from my bottom. I rolled off the skis and felt for damage. My pants were split open right up the seam to my crotch. I had two more layers under so that helped. I yelled up the hill, "I split my pants." They rolled on the snowy grass with laughter.

When I climbed back up the hill, we headed home. Maybe spring came early that year, as I do not remember any more adventurous ski trips that winter.

"Do Unto Others"

One day when I was in the fourth grade, in our two-room town school during the war years, we had visitors. Two men from the Coca-Cola Company came to our school. First, they handed out rulers to each of us. Good wooden rulers with a metal strip along the edge for a fine line. At each end of the ruler the name Coca-Cola was inscribed. In the middle were these words in an old English font, **"DO UNTO OTHERS AS YOU WOULD HAVE THEM DO UNTO YOU."** We were duly impressed.

Then the men came around to each one of us and handed out a small bottle of the Coca-Cola product. With a brief sales pitch, they opened up our bottles and we tried it. The strongest pop I ever had was an Orange Crush, until this time. We thought it was too strong, but we enjoyed the attention and the interruption from classwork.

It was a brilliant advertising gimmick, with a wonderful gift besides, but I am not sorry – Coca-Cola never caught on with me.

Same Bloodlines

It was the middle of the Depression in the 1930s. It was also the middle of the Dust Bowl drought years. As a result, the streetlights turned on in the middle of the day because of all the dust in the air. It was a time of great stress. The small-town businesses suffered. The farmers were not making much money either.

It was during this time that Donald, my husband to be, was an active youngster about five years old. He wanted, in the worst way, a piece of rope to play with. He did not quite dare to ask his dad; he had heard the grown-ups talk about how tough it was to make a living. Then one day he had a brilliant idea. He would go see "Hardware Paul" across the street from the Gunness garage. Hardwood Paul would know what to do. Donald told him what was needed – a piece of rope. "That's no problem," Hardwood Paul said, as he cut the length of rope and told Donald he would just charge his dad. Somehow a pocketknife was added to the sale. One happy boy left to show his dad.

I did not hear what happened next, but this is what I was told. A phone call was made to Hardware Paul. The first question asked was, "Do you think I'm made of pure gold"?

The rope and the knife were returned. End of story. But maybe not …

Let us advance some years into the future. Donald's grandson, about the same age as Donald had been, also asked for a rope. Wherever the boy was, the rope followed behind. Someone said, "Same blood line."

Another story comes to mind. Sometime later, Don and I went to the livestock auction in Sisseton, South Dakota. The animals were herded into the selling arena, with the auctioneer in charge. The animals were put through the gates to the arena to be sold and then herded out the opposite gates. It played out like clockwork – very smooth.

Then the auctioneer announced they would be selling two bulls, one at a time. The bulls looked identical. The gate to the arena was opened, but the first bull refused to enter. We all watched as they tried to get the bull to go through the gate. Finally he entered the arena. There had been about twenty minutes of struggle with the bull. After he was sold, the gates were opened for the second bull. The same thing happened. He refused to enter the arena.

Sitting in front of us were two older ranchers. The one turned to the other and said, "Same bloodline."

We can see that, whether people or animals, character traits are passed from one generation to another.

Part Two **Family Stories**

A Bright New Day

As the old song goes, "What a difference a day makes!"

It was a glorious day, a very special day, a day long awaited. When we turned on the switch at the power pole in the yard, the whole house became flooded with light! Electricity had finally arrived on our farm. The year was 1948.

We had florescent lights shining over the dining room table, it was almost too bright. Instead of two kerosene lamps, one on the kitchen wall and the other on the dining room table, we were now flooded with light. We had ceiling fixtures and plug-ins in every room and the pole in the yard covered our farmyard with light.

Gone were the days of cleaning and filling the lamps and lanterns for the barn each Saturday. My job! The Maytag washing machine motor was changed from gasoline to electric. There were no more exhaust fumes from the hose at the kitchen door and blown back into the kitchen. And the potatoes! No more baked potatoes in the oven on wash day. Because of the association, it was years before I could enjoy a baked potato.

An electric well pump was installed, and water was pumped to the milk cows with drinking cups by their stanchions. It was a new life. An electric refrigerator and a combination wood and electric stove were installed.

The times changed and life became easier. Through the years, many improvements were added. A few years later, my brother built a beautiful modern home on the farm.

With the addition of milking machines, my life became much better. Entering high school, I no longer had to milk cows before school. No longer did anyone call us, "Stinky farm kids from the country."

It was the beginning of a whole new era, the result of electricity coming to the country across the whole U.S.A. So, when you turn on that light switch, don't take it for granted.

Electricity was a wonderful gift from God.

My Mother's Swedish Meatballs

T here my mother stood by the stove, making her Swedish Meatballs. She knew how because Mother was born and raised in Sweden, immigrating to the United States in 1914 as a seventeen-year-old girl.

But now she was listening to her college student daughter, home for the weekend, in her farm home in Minnesota. I watched her as she prepared the meatballs for dinner: two eggs mixed in a bowl with a fork with just enough milk – she never measured. She always knew how much she needed. Next, the fresh breadcrumbs were added from her homemade bread. Breadcrumbs were absorbed in the milk and egg mixture, with salt and pepper seasoning. The ground beef was added and thoroughly mixed. Sometimes she also added freshly ground pork.

With a frying pan on the stove, it was time to create her Swedish meatballs. Taking two tablespoons in her hands, Mother began her beautiful hand symphony. Taking just enough meat mixture in a spoon, she transferred the mixture from spoon to spoon, turning each time to form her perfectly rounded meatballs. She may have turned each one six to seven times, but I was not counting. I stood mesmerized by the rhythmic poetry of her hands. She continued until the frying pan was full. The heat was turned on, and the meatballs started to brown. They were continually turned in the pan to form perfectly browned meatballs on all sides. Then they gently simmered with the cover on until thoroughly cooked. A flour and water mixture was made next, smooth with absolutely no lumps.

With the drippings, and the boiled potato water drained into the frying pan, Mother made the perfect gravy.

The meatballs and gravy, mashed potatoes, and home-canned corn or peas, plus bread and butter, and I will guess, as I do not remember, fluffy tapioca pudding topped with strawberry preserves for dessert, the meal was ready. It was a meal fit for a king and this hungry girl home from school.

All the food was home grown, and it showed my mother's artistry in action, making the meatballs and all the rest of the meal.

It was her testimony of her love for family.

It was her life, serving others, it was her life.

One-Button Overalls

I t was in the heart of the Depression in the '30s. Times were very hard. The banks everywhere went broke and the investors all lost savings, including my parents.

My dad hauled a trainload stock-car full of feeder pigs to the stock market in South St. Paul, Minnesota. There he had to pay extra to cover the freight costs. What year it was, I do not remember hearing. But there was not enough money for Dad to pay for new school clothes.

There was a family man in town whose hearing was destroyed in the trenches in France during WWI. He was also a rural mail carrier, so he had a pension and salary. It must have been terribly hard to do, but my father asked him if he would loan him $25 for school clothes. I think there were three children in school at that time in our house.

The mail order was sent to Sears Roebuck in Minneapolis. At that time the catalog had three different qualities of goods. One was the best and most expensive; the next one was cheaper and of less quality; and the last was the cheapest. My older brother got the cheapest overalls with only a one-button pocket on the bib. The kids whose families were on welfare got the most expensive three-button pocket overalls. Such humiliation.

There was a bully in the school who teased my brother about his one-pocket overalls. One of the older boys came to his rescue and the bully stopped.

I am sure that these stories are multiplied many times over in all of our small towns. Evidence of it was all the farm auctions, with many pulling up roots and sometimes heading for California.

Times were hard, but we made it. We paid our farm mortgage in the early 40's, when times were better, and Dad could afford more than three-button overalls.

The Threshing Crew

I remember vividly that every year in August, when I was a child, the huge steam engine threshing machine would lumber loudly, with a cloud of dust, into our driveway. It was positioned the day before needed to be ready for the oat and barley harvest. We belonged to a round of farmers who worked the harvest fields together. I think there were six to eight farmers each year who brought their team of horses to our farm, with wagons and hay racks ready to gather and move the shocks of grain to the steam operated threshing machine. Each bundle was forked one at a time into the thresher.

The threshing machines were huge and long. If you drive in Minnesota lake country, you may still see them standing as sentinels on the hilltops, not needed anymore with the invention of the combine that is still used today. With their outstretched long spout, that once poured straw into straw piles, the empty long-necked machines remind me of prehistoric mammals that one time roamed the hills where we lived.

This is how threshing worked. The man with the steam engine arrived about six each morning. He needed to start the fire in the fuel box, replenish the water to create the steam, and then come to the house for breakfast. He always wanted fried potatoes (which he did not get). My mother complained, "Why couldn't he eat breakfast at home"? With preparing two lunches and two main meals for the men, she had enough to do. The men would all work hard in the summer heat and pull out their red handkerchiefs to wipe the grime and sweat off their faces. They needed to be well fed.

Two at a time, one on each side, the horses and wagons edged toward the threshing rig and the men pitched the bundles, one at time, into the hopper. As each load of bundles was emptied, another two wagons took their places. It continued on all day, only to be stopped for food or a drink of water, until evening.

I want to tell you about Mother's work. She baked a number of loaves of bread the day before. There were no plastic bags or freezers yet. A metal-lined bread box and cover were under the worktable in Mother's kitchen. Morning coffee was hauled to the men in a coaster wagon. The coffee was made in the 50-cup enamel coffee pot, with sandwiches and cookies in the morning, and sandwiches and cake in the afternoon.

After the morning snack, we had to hurry to start the noon dinner. I was given a fork and a pail, then instructed to go to the garden to dig new potatoes. The plants could not be pulled up yet, so we dug around the outside of the plants and filled our pails. Some carrots were also pulled and some tomatoes picked. Earlier, Mother had started a pot roast in the oven. I scraped the new potatoes and carrots. Then I put the leaves into the dining room table and set it for twelve.

There was no break until the dishes were washed and it was time to prepare the afternoon coffee and snack. Then a repeat performance of the morning agenda. The men were always happy to see me. After I returned from the coffee service, Mother and I sat down to have a sandwich and a cup of coffee (with sugar and cream of course) – our one break in the day.

The evening meal preps began. I do not remember much, as I was getting too tired. Some of the men went home for supper and chores, so there was not as much food prepared. It was a full day for everyone. Sometimes the harvest took more than one day, so we repeated the events again. Everyone hoped it would not rain and usually it did not.

The whole crew moved to another farm when the threshing was completed at our place. This continued until harvest was finished.

There was a spirit of comradery and friendship between the farmers. It was harvest time and all were glad. My dad always had a smile on his face on that day because of the good crops.

A Found Poem

(Introduction by Karla Smart-Morstad)

Found poems are what their name indicates. They are paragraphs, sentences, phrases, or lists found in writing. Just as they are, they make a poem. A found poem. A newspaper, letter, or advertisement – any source of writing – can offer a found poem.

Alice found a poem about Knute Gunness (Donald's great-grandfather) while reading an unpublished Gunness family history written by Syvert Gunness (Donald's uncle) years ago. The images are powerful. For Alice, the paragraph was a poem. It reveals purpose and industry. It shows the creativity and contribution of Knute Gunness, an early businessman in Abercrombie, North Dakota. It illuminates one of Alice Gunness' topics – that generation of immigrants worked to better their lives as a foundation for future generations.

I corrected spelling, and, using all the words and punctuation from the prose paragraph, spaced the writing into a found poem.

Knute Gunness and The Gunness Blacksmith Shop
a found poem
Syvert Gunness (date unknown)

Knute was a very capable, ingenious blacksmith.
Practically all of the machinery
were built and fabricated with his homemade tools.

The feed mill was powered by a large
multi-vein windmill. The mill consisted of

two large circular stones, one stationary and the other
turned by means of large handmade wooden gear wheels.

These stones are on the Gunness farm.

After the corn was crushed or ground by these stones,
the ground meal was put through a handmade separator.
All of the tools were handmade:
chisels, tongs, vises forge, bellows,
turning lathe—wood and iron.

He made drills and taps and dies for a thread cutting—
these are now in the Fort Abercrombie State Historical Museum.
Light and heavy forge work, horseshoeing, wagon work,
plowshare sharpening, fabricating galvanized iron cisterns
are but a few of the many types of work
carried on in the shop.

The Winter Lumberjack

Oh! If only I had asked more questions! If only I had listened more carefully! I barely remember my dad telling about spending his winters, in the Northwoods of Minnesota, working as a lumberjack when he came to this country. He was working to save money to buy a farm.

It was a rough and tough life in logging camps during the second decade of the twentieth century. Survival of the fittest was the rule of the winter. The company had to know that he would <u>stay</u> and know how to work before he was hired. But he was hired and worked a number of winters in the logging camps.

There was a variety of jobs to do: sawing down trees; using horses to drag logs to the hill overlooking the river; and walking the logs in the river to keep the logs going straight as they floated in the current of the spring flooded water.

My dad worked with his partner to saw down the hardwood trees. The trees were mostly oaks used to make beautiful furniture. The loggers used a "Swede saw," or a cross-cut saw, with a blade about six feet long. The saw had handles on each end. It was tricky working to have one man on each side of the tree. One logger would saw, and the other helped hold the saw in place but did not push as that would cause the saw to become bound-up in the tree trunk. When that happened it was difficult to get the saw out. There was a steady rhythm in the sawing until the tree was cut down. The next step was trimming the branches and sawing the log to the right length. And so it was, the lumberjacks kept moving from tree to tree until spring.

When the season ended, the loggers all bought new clothes, burned up what they had worn all winter, took a kerosene bath to rid themselves of lice and mites, and then caught a train back to civilization—Minneapolis and St. Paul.

A Frightful Christmas

I t was a miserable day for Christmas. The sky was overcast and cloudy with a marauding northwest wind barreling through the yard. A few snowflakes added to the gloom.

Church services were in the afternoon; everyone was used to that. My dad came in at noon after feeding the cattle and asked if we were going to church. My mother announced that she was staying home that day. Nothing more was said, but I wondered about it. My next older brother and I were the only two kids living at home and I was about ten years old.

At that time the women and children sat on the left side of the church and the men and boys sat on the right. I was feeling lonesome for my mother as I did not sit with my dad, but I cannot remember anything more. Looking back, I do remember sitting in church and looking over all the other mothers, but my mom was the best looking of all. My dad confirmed this years later on the morning of my wedding: He looked over the breakfast table on that day and said of his three daughters, my mother was the prettiest of us all on her wedding day.

We arrived home to find my mother in an exhausted frenzy. While we were gone, we had a dreaded chimney fire. The pipe from the kitchen stove followed horizontally to the chimney, about four and a half feet. A chimney fire was always greatly feared. My mother grabbed a box of baking soda and poured it on the flames in the kitchen stove. She then went outside to check the chimney, and saw sparks and flames shooting up into the sky in the high wind. As she hurried back into the house, she heard crackling sounds coming from above where the four and a half stretch of stove pipe was red hot. She climbed up the stairs into the attic in our small house and looked in the crawl space where she saw flames. There was a small fire burning in the eaves above the stove pipe. She hurried back downstairs and grabbed a pail of water from the kitchen. She climbed back upstairs and poured it on the flames. She made several more trips until she was satisfied that the fire was out.

By the time we returned from church, she was all in. But her staying home from church kept our home from burning up. "I had a premonition that something was going to happen. That's why I didn't go to church," she told us.

Chimney fires were a constant worry with the burning of wood in the winter. Creosote would build up in the stove pipes every so often so the pipes would have to be cleaned about three times a winter. The fires were allowed to die down and the pipes were hauled out into the yard, cleaned and hauled back into place. B-r-r-r the house got cold! If you have ever lived through a chimney fire, the smell is something so powerful you will never forget. It is a distinct odor that no other fire can produce. It would permeate the house and you never forgot.

Thank God for my mother who listened and heeded the warning that was sent that day. She saved our house, our home, and our belongings. Peace reigned later at Christmas that year but a little fear always lurked in the background.

Model T's

M odel T cars were popular with the high school crowd in the 1940s. It was a cheap form of transportation and the older set were driving newer model cars. For those too young for military service during the war, finding a Model T in some hidden corner in a farm shed was no small deal.

My husband Donald's best friend, a couple of years older, was working. He saved up his money and brought home a Model T. All it took was five gallons of gas for $1.00, scrounged between friends, to fill up at the filling station. They were on their way to Wahpeton, North Dakota, on Saturday afternoon. With two movie theaters in town, they made their choices carefully. For the price of a ticket, about fifteen to twenty-five cents, they could take in an afternoon matinee or two and stay for the evening show as well.

Coming out from the theater, the friends headed for the diner next door for hamburgers, fries, and malts. The cost was under fifty cents. Not bad for a one-day deal!

Do you remember King Leo's the first drive-in in Fargo, North Dakota? Seventeen cents comes to mind for a small hamburger and fries.

Time moved on until coming home from Korea and college, Donald drove a new Chevy Bel Aire, 1954 model. It was an awful two-tone salmon color. Over the years, vehicles changed and improved and continued to cost more money.

Now moving ahead fifty or sixty years, we have a family member with a PhD in electrical engineering. Can you imagine what he is doing? He is designing computer chips for the components of DRIVERLESS CARS!

What a very long way from the Model T!

Church Giggles

I s there anything more difficult than getting the giggles in church? The pew was just vibrating. How do you stop, along with your three daughters? My husband, Don, reached around my shoulders and tapped our youngest daughter on her shoulder, but it did not help.

A man volunteered to sing in church – a bachelor with a good job in a neighboring community. He came from a ranch in remote western North Dakota. Maybe he had been listening to too many country western songs and singing along. He said that as a child he sang along with his mother at the piano. They sang old hymns together. He sang without accompaniment. Not only did he have a decidedly western twang, it was flat besides. Maybe it was "Rock of Ages" or "What a Friend We Have in Jesus." I think he underestimated our abilities to appreciate good music. For thirty-five years, our pastor's wife had led the choir and played the organ. It was church music at its best. She had a well-trained voice.

But that was yesterday and our new pastor agreed to have the gentleman sing. It was bad, and the longer he sang, the funnier it got. Oh my, what to do? My husband was embarrassed by all our bad behavior. We were terribly guilty of giggling but could not help it. Sometimes when you are not supposed to laugh, it gets even funnier! So it was, one Sunday morning in our church in our little hometown.

Chapter Two

The World Around Us

An Unexpected Dinner

It was a lovely late winter day, balmy for February in North Dakota. Our pastor friend came for a visit, so we were drinking coffee. Some wild turkeys were walking by the yard, a few deer were munching on corn screenings Don put out, and a pair of squirrels were chasing each other up and down the trees. A black cat was sitting on the snow drift in front of the house, under the tree, sunning herself.

All of a sudden, the squirrel, with great conviction, ran headlong for the cat and attacked. There was a twisting and turning and rolling and tussling in the snow. Round and round they went, just a blur. Suddenly, all was quiet. The cat picked up the dead squirrel by the neck and dragged it between her front feet to her house in the nearby shed.

We were flabbergasted at what had just happened. A squirrel attacking a cat! Never!

About an hour later the big cat lumbered by slowly through the yard with bulging sides and a look of great satiation on her face. A while later, the tomcat also emerged. "Stuffed to the gills," as the old saying goes. I think they had a good long nap after that.

This brings to mind the old adage, "Know your opponent before you attack."

My Pepper

When he was whelped, he was in the last litter of purebred Border Collie puppies that we raised to sell. It was time to quit raising puppies, as the children were gone from home. It was time to say goodbye to the puppies at eight weeks.

A little side note. It is always better to charge for puppies rather than to give them away, regardless of their heritage. People take better care of things they have paid for.

I think there were five puppies in this litter, and he was the biggest. I loved his disposition. He seemed gentler and less rambunctious than the rest. At eight weeks it was time to let them go to good homes. Border Collies are working dogs, so a rural setting is the best. They do not thrive well in town, as they are very ambitious and want to work. They are also good watchdogs and help to keep the raccoons, skunks, and other varmints from the farmyard. They will always let their owner know when someone turns into the driveway.

It so happened that only four puppies sold. I was happy and the pup was happy to be home. A roly-poly, cuddly puppy went to a long-legged teenager with still a lot to be learned.

It happened that Peter came home to visit about New Year's. We had four or five inches of snow on the ground, where the wind had not whipped it free. He was driving the four-wheel-drive pickup through the snow over to the shop. Pepper, named for his sprinkle of dark spots on top of his muzzle, was happily keeping Peter company in the snow. Somehow, Pepper slipped under the wheel and was run over. Heart-broken, Peter came carrying him in his arms and set him down in the back hall. We felt him all over, but did not seem to find any broken bones, though he seemed lifeless.

We called the vet to ask his advice. Since it was Sunday afternoon, he was not eager to meet us at the clinic. "Give him a couple of aspirin and let him rest to see what happens. He may have internal injuries." I asked him what to do if he needed to empty his bladder and this is what he said, "Put a good piece of plastic down with an old towel underneath the dog. He will automatically relieve himself when it is time. Call me tomorrow to tell me how he is doing."

Pepper was being as sweet as ever. He lay on his side and rested. Everything was going okay until we tried to leave. He whimpered and cried and did not let up. We pulled his plastic sheet into the family room and everything was fine, but when we tried to leave him to go to bed, the crying continued. We agreed to place his sheet on the floor beside the bed. "It won't hurt the carpet any." Not a peep was heard from him for the rest of the night. Sometime later, I awoke to smell urine so that was a good sign. I pulled out the wet towel and bedded him down again.

When he awoke in the morning, he was unable to get up, so he just rested that day and the next. I kept him company lest he cry. I had some mending to do that day, so I carried my sewing machine to the desk in the back hall. He happily stayed by my side all day. The next day he got up and toddled a little. He was stiff and sore, and he walked like an old man for several weeks.

By the time February rolled around, he needed some exercise and so did we. We started walking together every day on the road past our farm. As the weeks went on, we taught him to heel, sit, walk, and stay, and later to roll over and play dead. He wanted to please and be obedient and learn all we had to teach him.

Pepper was my dog, and he showed his love, obedience, and loyalty every day.

He was our tool to keep our farm free from varmints and critters, and we loved him dearly.

Catching the Sheep

My husband, Donald, told me this story. When he returned home from Korea, he attended North Dakota Agricultural College, now North Dakota State University. A professor of animal husbandry told the class, "I asked my students to write an essay on sheering sheep. The student who got an A on the assignment was the one who wrote, 'First, you have to catch the sheep.'"

This real-life story has many applications. How many times a day do you have to catch the sheep?

When the children are soon out the door for school, do they get a hug?

When your husband tells you about his day, whether before he leaves or returning home, do you tell him how much he is loved?

When you answer the phone, do you smile because it helps?

When you face interruptions all day long, do you think how to handle them?

Are you catching your sheep?

Do the cares of the day come with you as you enter your home?

Are we scolding more than praising?

As a wife and mother, are we willing to catch the sheep or scatter them?

There is a time for catching and a time for letting go.

Lord, grant us grace to continually know when to be catchers of sheep.

Isella

Her name was Isella, a Spanish name for a Spanish dog. She was a cousin of the poodle family with hair, rather than fur, that did not shed. She was all white with a big, bushy tail that curled up right over her back. The up-turned tail showed she was purebred. She weighed about fifteen pounds. Isella belonged to our daughter Sarah and was her dearly loved companion. She was an exceptionally well-behaved lap dog.

One Christmas Eve, Sarah arrived home and brought Isella with her. They had been bumped from four flights between Denver and Fargo. Sarah was tired. She was carrying her overnight bag, Christmas presents, and a dog carrier. She forgot and put the dog carrier on the conveyer through the X-ray machine. She called us, in a panic, fearing she had done something terrible to her beloved Isella. "Is she going to die, Mom"? she asked. I did not know for sure, but I said, "Low levels of X-rays would be about like having a broken bone X-rayed." Much relieved, Sarah and Isella arrived home none the worse for wear.

After Sarah and Geir married, and had two children, Isella was replaced as number one. I always thought she had a sad look after the children came. When the children were in bed for the night, Isella jumped up to snuggle with Sarah, as if to say, "Finally now it's my turn."

Having had Border Collies on the farm, it was a different experience to live with a lap dog. When Don and I went to visit, Isella was my girl! One time when she saw me get out of the car, she was so excited that she ran in circles coming into the house. I sat down and greeted her. Isella then ran into the kitchen and all of a sudden, she was so excited she peed. When she realized what she had done, she turned with an incredulous look on her face, as if to say, "I didn't do that, did I"?

Isella was well-loved and gave much love in return.

Autumn Leaves

"The autumn leaves flit by my window,
The autumn leaves of red and gold.

But I love you most of all, my darling,
When autumn leaves start to fall."

The yearly drives to see the fall colors gave great joy! We took several trips to see them all, as the different trees colored at different times. As we traveled, the sun felt good through the car windows. We needed sunny and clear days to see the fall beauty best.

Early on in September, the brilliant crimson leaves of the sumac bushes lined the highways for miles. The mature trees were still in their green garb. What a contrast!

Several weeks later the trees were beginning to color. The tall elms of shining gold blended with tawny ash trees, and the blazing maples became the spotlight with brilliant colors of red and orange. The clusters of poplar trees, or poples as they are commonly called, were showing off their gold, too. The kaleidoscope of rich colors lined the hillsides as we drove on. The maples always dominated the landscape, whether they stood alone in full glory or mixed with the other colors of fall. The show was spectacular! Birch trees with their paper white trunks were covered with golden coins fluttering in the autumn breeze. With each day, leaves began to float to earth or shed abruptly to the winds of fall, some leaving early and some late, with the bare skeletons of branches silhouetted against the sky on the hilltops.

"But I love you most of all, my darling,
When autumn leaves start to fall."

As we drove among the hills of home, ponds and lakes mirrored October's "Bright Blue Weather." Along the swamps stood clumps of stately Tamarac evergreen trees, their needles turning to gold also. They are the only evergreen to change their color and drop their needles in the fall. In nature there is always an exception to every rule. So it is by faith alone we find God, the creator of everything.

"But I love you most of all, my darling,
When autumn leaves start to fall."

We motored on that day to a lovely red oak grove. I used to catch a glimpse of them every day on the school bus. The red oak colored a dark, deep, rich burgundy. Not only that, but the leaves hang on the trees all winter without losing much color.

So ends my ode to autumn, when the snowflakes also begin to fall.

"But I love you most of all, my darling,
When autumn leaves start to fall."

Bee Sting Therapy

He asked me so nicely, I could not say, "No." My husband planned to move some honey bees to a new location that evening. He asked me to come along and hold a flashlight for him, so he could see to load the beehives, which were on the pallets, with a Bobcat loader.

It was still light when we left the house for Don to pick up the twenty pallets and place them on the flatbed truck, so I just watched. I was wearing a thin pair of anklets as I was only going to hold the light! For precaution we would always tape our jeans and overalls with masking tape at our ankles, to make sure the bees could not crawl up our legs. We had on gloves and bee suits with white cotton tops and mesh hoods to put over our faces. Bees seem to go for the eyes when they are flying.

As we worked the night came on. It reminded me of the poem *The Creation*, "It was blacker than a hundred midnights down in the cypress swamps." (James Weldon Johnson) We drove to the new bee yard location. There was a long field of sunflowers close by for pollination. We parked on the edge of a neighboring pasture, as directed by the landowner. Don began unloading the pallets, four colonies per pallet, with a usual amount of 60,000 bees per colony. I was holding the light as he backed-up the Bobcat and turned to set the pallets in a row.

Suddenly the wheel of the Bobcat hit a hole in the ground, and it started to tip. Two of the colonies, stacked three boxes high, fell over. We were in trouble. We had to pick up the honeycombs and place them back in the hives. The ground was littered with angry, crawling bees. 60,000 times two equals 120,000 bees. And where were the two queens? Hopefully, they were still in the torn-open hives.

The bees were crawling all over, when they discovered my ankles and the thin socks they could sting right through. If one bee stings you, the others smell the venom and start to sting also. My ankles were beginning to feel hotter and hotter with successive stings as we proceeded to pick up the combs and put them in the hives. The bees on the ground would find their way back to the hives in the morning light. Finally, we were able to pick up the hives and place them back on the pallet.

We finished the rest of the unloading, drove the Bobcat onto the trailer behind the truck, and drove home. It was all in a night's work for the beekeeper—the unexpected sometimes does happen.

After we drove home, I pulled off my socks and counted over thirty stings on both ankles. But, after the stinging event, I never have had any more arthritis problems, as before with my ankles, no pain whatsoever to this day. So, it was a fair trade for me! Using the venom for pain relief is called BEE STING THERAPY.

Bee sting therapy for pain has been used for hundreds and thousands of years and it does work! Even when it is not planned!

Bringing the Bees to School

For a number of years, Don and I went to Wahpeton Central School to bring a demonstration about honeybees, at the invite of the teacher. It was delightful with about sixty second graders gathered in one room to hear our presentation. We would show greatly enlarged pictures of honeybees with the Queen and the workers in their hive. Second graders are a very good audience. They listened intently.

Don showed them the "smoker," which when lit, calms the bees so that they can be worked. Also, he showed a hive tool that the beekeeper holds in his hands as he works the bees. Don brought along a honeycomb with bees that were just hatching. The bees are in their little six-sided cells for twenty-one days before they eat themselves out. They are not able to sting for ten days after they come out, so they were not dangerous. Anyone who wanted could hold a live bee in their hands. We taught them that bees are our friends because of all the good they do in pollenating our fruits, vegetables, and nuts.

Next the big excitement of the program: I had Don give me a bee sting on my hand. Then I went about the room showing them the stinger. The children watched as the two little muscles pumped the venom into my skin. The kids were in awe.

Then we taught them how to carefully remove the stinger, scraping it sideways. If you try to get it out by pulling it from the top, you squeeze the venom into your body. That can be dangerous. The highlight of the day, after I walked around, was when a little worried second grader asked me, "Are all those other spots on your hand where he stung you before?" I quickly answered, "Oh no, those are grandma spots." It was a thrill each year to teach about honeybees to the classroom of children. They all had a honey stick full of honey to bring home. All wrote the nicest thank you letters which are very priceless to us. Precious memories!

My Favorite Birch Trees

My home farmyard has several trees. The first two trees Donald and I planted were paper birch saplings. We had no lawn or trees on our rural property, just the shell of our new home being built on the black soil.

My brother-in-law called one day in our first June together in 1956. He told us that the railroad company right-of-way adjoining my dad's land in Richville, Minnesota would be burned off the next day. Two paper birches would also be burned. Birch trees are precious to me, as my Swedish name Bjorklund means birch land or birch grove. We jumped at the chance to get these two young saplings by digging them up that evening and transporting them to our new home. One was a single tree, but the other was a clump birch with five trees growing together. They are huge and spectacular sixty years later. In the fall, the leaves turn the most beautiful shade of gold. Their round leaves remind me of gold coins shining in the sun.

One tree sits west of the house, and the clump birch seems like it fills up the whole back yard. It arches over our house so we can see it even from our driveway in the front. We also have a European small leaf linden, two American large leaf linden (basswood trees), and a gorgeous autumn blaze maple and Colorado blue spruce. A friend told me that basswood trees mean "welcome" and the evergreens "come again." You can tell, I love trees. But, my favorite are the paper birch trees Don and I first planted in our empty yard.

The Lake Alice Surprise

When the calm, quiet, low waters of summer become a wild torrent of rushing overland flooding, spreading out for miles, you know the Red River of the North is on the rampage. After sixty years of watching and waiting to see the river come up in the spring, every year is still a new experience. If the winter snows are light, the flooding will be minimal, but the opposite may also come true.

The rate and amount of snow to melt are the deciding factors. Living on a river farm is an ever-new experience from year to year. Most of the years, the river flows into our bottom land where it ran centuries ago. The amount of water varies from year to year and determines the amount of water filling what we call Lake Alice. It is about a half mile wide, and long, and twenty to thirty feet deep in places. It usually stays high for two plus weeks or more, and then drains out, like a bathtub, when the river recedes. When the river floods in early spring, it usually dries out in time for planting and is not a problem. Flooding in the middle of summer, as a result of severe thunderstorms, can destroy a crop or certainly lower the yield.

It was so much fun to watch the migrating spring water birds arrive. The first to arrive were Merganser Ducks, and then the Wood Ducks followed by Mallards. Small family-size groups would land and rest and feed on corn or soybeans left from the last fall's harvest. They would tip upside down and dive underwater to gather their meals. They were able to stay underwater an amazingly long time. I would sit at my desk chair and count until they returned topside.

One year we had a most unusual experience—the arrival of a flock of Whistling Swans. With white all over, and black beaks, and black webbed feet, they were gorgeous. They were much larger than the other birds. There were about twenty-five to thirty swans. My bird book said they were the only swans who held their necks straight up and down without a curve. They are considered quite rare.

The Whistling Swans seemed to float effortlessly over the water. The mates in the group stayed close together. In the three weeks they were there, they did not make a sound. They reminded me of big, beautiful, fluffy white pillows, when they turned upside down to feed in the shallow water. I surely wondered why they were called Whistling Swans. One full-moon evening, as I was preparing for bed, I heard strange noises coming from Lake Alice. I opened my window. The Whistling Swans were easy to see in the water, making hauntingly beautiful, high pitched sounds all night long. Maybe it was the full moon; maybe they were saying goodbye; maybe they were encouraging each other for the long flight ahead; maybe they were praying to their heavenly Father for protection on their long flight to the northern tundra of Canada.

What a privilege it was to see the wildlife every year, but it was a special gift to hear the Whistling Swans. We remember that the Word says, "Every good and perfect gift comes down from the Father of Lights." (James 1:17, NKJV)

The Woodpecker

What parent has never been awakened in the middle of the night, not by a thunderstorm in progress overhead, but by the crying screams of a young child, frightened by the thunder and lightning? As the children crawled into bed beside us, my husband would calm them with this darling ditty, which his mother taught him when he was a small child. It goes like this:

"The woodpecker pecked out a little round hole
and made him a house in the telephone pole.
When the lightning flashed and the thunders rolled
he snuggled right down in his telephone pole."
(*The Woodpecker*, Elizabeth Madox Roberts, 1881-1941)

Finishing the poem, Don would say, "I always sleep best when it is thunder storming outside." Then he would roll over and go to sleep, and the rest of us would calm down and go to sleep, too.

I write this in memory of Don's mother, Adelia, who had a nice way with children.

A Night to Remember

Just when we residents of Riverview Place finished eating our evening meal, at 6:15 p.m. Friday, January 4, 2019, a man ran through the dining room shouting in a loud voice, "Evacuate immediately! There is a fire and you must evacuate the building. Go to the front entrance."

A story one resident told adequately describes our feelings at that moment. A resident said, "We had a fresh piece of white cake with frosting for dessert. I was so looking forward to eating it, and I only got two bites before we had to hurriedly leave. It was a large piece of cake, too."

We were herded out the door to the rental apartment building across the street. It was icy and slushy, and the temperature thirty degrees Fahrenheit with a light breeze. Thank God it was not any colder. We were not allowed to get our wraps. We were not allowed to use the elevators either.

In the neighboring apartment building, there were about a hundred people stuffed into two rooms. One was a nice, big eating and all-purpose room and the other was an entry room. It was cold sitting and waiting, as people kept coming and going out the front door. It took about three hours before the all clear sounded.

Some people called family and they were picked up. Others from Riverview apartments came in later and they were told to go to the chapel in the building the rest of us had left. But the chapel began filling up with smoke, so still more came to the apartments across the street. There were people with walkers and wheelchairs and others needing help. A bit of confusion all around. No one knew for sure the details of the fire except that it was Building C at Riverview.

Thank you, Heavenly Father, for providing a place so close so that we did not have to stay outside in our short sleeves. Thank you for all the staff who stayed late to help, and those who returned, and all the residents who helped.

Everyone sat patiently and quietly waited. Then the administrators came in and checked us off one-by-one. The staff also checked every room for residents. We had to all be accounted for.

One lady was already in bed sleeping at 6:30 in building A. When they brought her over, she was sitting in the entry room with her nightgown reaching her ankles and her parka on above. She is apparently a very quiet lady, but she had a pleased look on her face as if to say, "Oh, isn't this exciting!"

Next, we were asked if we had family to go to, or if we needed a hotel room. That worried us even more. Finally, at 8:30 we were given word that we could return to our apartments – everyone except those in building C which was now completely closed off. We later found out that there were four apartments that were severely damaged or destroyed and there was smoke damage throughout the building.

The following Monday, Riverview Residents gathered to give thanks to God for His provision. We did not have to be rousted out in the middle of the night. We were thankful that the fire had not been caused by a resident. We were all cared for, and everyone allowed to return, to sleep in our own beds that night. Thanks be to God.

What Else Happened that Night

First, there were reports from residents of a strong gas smell in the area of the Riverview C Building sometime before the dinner hour. It must have been about 6:00 p.m. when the night nurse went down to check out the smell. When she opened the door of the mechanical room, an explosion occurred, and fire started shooting out of the building. The fire department was called, and they came looking for the fire. They were on the street side of the out buildings and didn't see any flames. The same nurse ran through D and E buildings to reach the fire trucks. She told them to turn into the courtyard where they could see the flames shooting out into the sky. Five fire trucks arrived plus the Command Vehicle, twenty-two firemen and other support people from the ambulance and Salvation Army. According to the Fargo Forum, they had to call the gas company to shut off the gas in the yard before the fire was controlled. It completely or partially destroyed four rental units with major soot and smoke damage in the entire building.

There were several people in the C Building who needed to be evacuated. One of the CNAs was sent to the C building to get the residents out. The smoke started filling up the rooms and it was getting hard to see, as she raced through the halls banging on doors and ordering everyone out. Some she had to really help. She said it was very frightening.

Supper was a transition period as some people were milling around before going up to their apartments. But there were also many who had their pajamas on as well. The staff opened every apartment in the complex to look for people. Not everyone heard the alarms go off. Everyone was very thankful that all were safe and accounted for; a prayer service was held the following Monday to give thanks for all the blessing and answers to prayers.

It was a night to remember and hopefully will never happen again.

Spring Bloom

in just spring when the world is mud luscious and puddle wonderful
- e. e. cummings

From the Bible, "When the singing of the birds has come" we know the spring is here (Song of Solomon, 2:12, NKJV).

About the middle of April, when the first signs of life emerge, the tree blooms begin. Many people are not aware, except those whose allergies are flaring from the tree pollen carried on a spring breeze.

Each tree is different in its bloom. Some trees, like the Box Elder, a rather homely tree, sends forth the most extravagantly pale, green, dangling earrings. The Red Maple trees show a rosy glow or halo over their branches as they begin to bloom. All this bloom happens before the trees leaf out. The spring rains are much needed to soften the new buds and help to unfurl the leaves.

Have you stopped to breathe in the perfumed air? Such a grand combination of scent. First to bloom are the hardwood trees – oaks and elms, the pungent wild plums, the delicate odor of apple trees, and other fruit trees. Next come the Caragana hedges in the shelter belt and the heavy rich odor of the Russian olive trees. Each one says, "I'm here! I'm blooming! Smell me!"

The tree blooms are for the honeybees and other insects to gather pollen or bee bread. A queen bee lays up to 1500 eggs each day through the spring and summer months. It is vital that the baby bees, in the six-sided cells, are fed pollen for eight days. The larvae are then capped over and sealed with bee's wax, as they continue to develop into an adult bee after twenty-one days. The pollen is stored in the honeycombs in the brood section where the queen lays each egg in each cell. To continue providing pollen for baby bees in summer, two more trees bloom extravagantly. The European Linden and the native Basswood trees begin to bloom from July 1st to the 10th with a most exotic, heavy perfume in clusters of white flowers all over the trees. If you stand by the trees you may hear the bees hum as they collect pollen and honey.

Nature knows what is needed in all areas. In order for us to eat and enjoy many of the fruits and vegetables that are produced, honeybees and other insects are needed to pollinate blooms.

Nature knows how the food chain works and grows. We are dependent on all of God's gifts in nature. All things are given to us for our provision. Thanks be to God.

Pictures

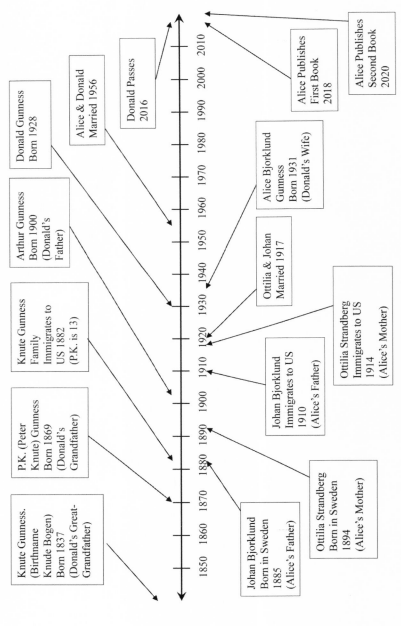

Donald and Alice (Bjorklund) Gunness Family Timeline

The Gunness workshop in Abercrombie, North Dakota
circa 1910. Knute Gunness built the windmill (a gristmill
used for milling grains) by hand in 1888. Left to right:
Clarence (Donald's uncle), P.K. (Donald's grandfather), John
(Donald's uncle), and Knute (Donald's great-grandfather).

Knute Gunness' family circa 1900. Seated: wife Kari, Knute (Donald's great-grandfather), Ryne (eldest daughter). Standing: Ingebricht, P.K. (Peter Knute, Donald's grandfather, who was about thirteen when they immigrated to the US), youngest daughter – name unknown.

P.K. and Randine Gunness family around 1920. Seated: P.K.,
Randine, John Clifford (WWI soldier). Standing: Syvert, Ruth,
Arthur (Donald's father), Helma, Clarence, Naomi (youngest).

P.K. Gunness blacksmithing in his shop circa 1930. (Note
the two racks of horseshoes hanging at the left of the picture,
an anvil in front of and the forge blasting behind him,
and a barrel of quenching water at the bottom right.)

Above: Donald and Alice on their wedding day, March 25, 1955.
Below: Alice and Donald sixty years later on
Donald's eighty-eighth birthday, 2016.

Alice at a meeting of the Riverview Writing Crew,
when publishing a book of her stories was nothing
more than that twinkle in her eye, 2017

Alice and granddaughter Silja celebrating Alice's eighty-fifth birthday and commemorating the publishing of her first book with a book-shaped birthday cake, 2019.

Alice addressing the crowd at one of her book signings, 2018.

Chapter Three

Our Family Stories

Family Letters Back to Sweden 1933-35

A few months back I received an email from my cousin, Håkan Persson, in Storvik, Sweden. It turns out he is a descendant of my father's sister Marta. He sent me three letters from my parents which he translated from Swedish into English for my reading. The letters were sent in December of 1933-34-35.

I am impressed with my father giving so much detail in his letters. The letter writers tell about the Great Depression of the 1930s, and even include mention of my birth in 1933. These letters are a treasure to me.

December 3, 1933, Richville, Minnesota

Dear Sister and Brother in law with family,

I must thank you for the letters and the gift I got since last time I wrote. It was sad that it went so fast with Olof. We saw in the newspaper that he fell on his Motorcycle and got hurt so bad that he passed away before getting to the hospital in Bolinas, so it's weird that it can go so fast sometimes. I remember him since last winter we stayed at your place when he slept over with us.

We got us a little girl 20th of July (Alice) so now we have three girls and three boys. Allan and Gunhild, they go to high school, it's the second year now. Recent year we rented two rooms there, so they came home only on Saturday and went back on Sunday. This year they go to school by car with a neighboring boy, so it's better now when they can come back every day, if not too much snow. We have had snow and cold weather since last November, so it's going to be a long winter. We got no rain during the summer period, nor Autumn, so everything is as dry as it could be. The trees dried and died, the lake dries up too. It gets worse and worse every year. We got a bad harvest this summer, the seed dried so I harvest the small piece I got. The corn was better, since it can resist the dry period better.

We have also had disease and bad luck this summer as well, but it could've been worse as well, since Gunhild got sepsis in one of her legs in June, so we had to take her to the doctor every day for a period until she got better. And I also hurt my eye at home, it was in July, so I had to go to the doctor, but it got worse instead of better, so I had to look for an eye specialist in Fergus Falls, about 6 Swedish mil from here, so we had to rent a car again and I need to go to him every second day for about 2 months, so twice a week, and now only once a week, so I hope it's soon been healed. I could hardly see something for about 2 months, as also the other eye got inflamed. I had such a terrible pain, so I thought I'll go totally crazy, since I couldn't sleep for a long period, you don't value the health as long as you have it. We have miserable times here in the States for farmers and workers. On the farm we have enough to eat, so we don't have to starve, but if there won't be a change soon, then all the farmers have to leave their farms, because on the revenues we pay such high taxes excluding interest rates and so on. I can't give regards from Olof's (St Paul) and Anton's (Ohio, Stenbenville) families as I haven't heard anything for a while.

Dearest regards to all of you and we wish you a Merry Christmas and a Happy New Year from all of us.

Sincerely Johan Bjorklund

December 1, 1934, Richville, Minnesota

Dear relatives (Ottilia writes this time)

I have long time considered to write to Johan's only sister Marta, but now it happens. How do you have it home, back in old beloved Sweden, hopefully good. We all have a good health for the moment and wish you the same.

I don't remember if Johan wrote since you got my last letter with the photos, thanks anyway, it was much appreciated, so nice photos. So large farms you seem to have, large acreages too. Now another son left your home, and with only one girl home to help you. I guess you have so much to do on such a large farm, but the good boys perhaps can help a lot. Our children have also come to grow, Gunhild and Allan are 15 and 16 years old now, and go in third year of high school in Perham, a town about 2 Swedish mil from here, so we don't get that much help from them, only on the summer period, Martha and Harry goes to school here, Clarence and Alice are home with me still, how time goes fast. Gunhild and Allan would love to write to the cousins back home in Sweden, but it's such bad that they can't either speak or write Swedish, any of them, it's hardly any Swedes left here now, so we seldom speak Swedish. My sister lives nearby in St Paul and she has a daughter who's doing all the writing and that way we hear from them quite often.

Well, soon it's Christmas again, it's not snowing every day, but it surely looks like Christmas already. It was a really nice autumn we had over here. Johan got all the work done, I mean plowing and such things. Do you suffer anything from dry summers back home in Sweden? Here it has been really dry for many years now, so soon everything dries away, forest and everything dries. It's really bad times to live in America nowadays, but you can't expect better in a country where the Republicans rule and a large amount of the population don't know anything. In August the Bjorklunds (Olof's family) from St Paul were here and it was really nice, all their boys are grown now. Anton, the oldest, took his own family with him as well. Johan speaks often about Sweden and follows what's happening in Sweden from the Swedish News Magazine, and also the news from home. We hope and look forward to your reply.

Also we wish you a Merry Christmas and a Happy New Year.

Dearest Ottilia, Johan and the children

December 5, 1935 Richville, Minnesota

Dear Sister and Brother in Law with family

Thousands of thanks for the nice birthday gift that I got, it was really kind of you, but you shouldn't send so much, particularly since we can't send something back to you. Have you or any of your girls woven it? I got it when we were just getting the autumn harvest to the barn. so therefore, I'm in a rush to reply to you. We got a great hay-harvest this summer, even if we had bd weather, so it was a lot of work with this, and it has been the same conditions all summer, we got good harvest of everything but wheat, that was bad, but it was big difference compared to 1932-33-34, then it was too dry. 1934 it was so dry we hardly got anything at all. It feels nice to have enough now again, even if it was a lot of hard work with it. We have harvest everything ourselves. Farmers gets such small payments when we sell it, so you can't afford to rent staff.

Allan, he won a free trip to the State Expedition in St Paul the last days of August so he was at Olof and his family. He was there ten days so it was interesting for him to see everything over there. He and Gunhild goes to college this year again, it's the last year, it's seventeen persons in the class from our town and it's seventeen kilometers from here, but it's great that they can come home every evening. Allan, he broke his collarbone in October so he couldn't help us hardly with anything for over a month. Marta, Harry and Clarence, they go to school here so we only have Alice here at home now during the days. Ottilia got a letter from Kristina (wife of Hans Bjorklund, brother of Johan) who had visited Lotbodarne (Kilafors, Sweden) and she mentioned also that your girls are married too and also that Per-Erik's son (brother of Johan) also had been married, so we heard they take over the farm, s Per-Erik better find new home.

From Anton (Bjorklund, brother of Johan who moved to Ohio) we haven't heard for a long time. I have written a few letters that I haven't gotten reply of, so I wonder I have insulted him, which I'm not aware about. Have you heard from him?

It looks really worrying out in the world again and it looks like it's going to be a World War again. I read in the papers that you have good times in Sweden, since population is informed, even the American papers write that Sweden is the best place on Earth. I do not remember if I have said thanks for the photos I got from you, it looks so nice so I get homesick when I see it.

We are all healthy and wish you the same.

So I should stop for this time and once again say thank you for the nice present. My dearest regards and wishing you a Merry Christmas and a Happy New Year from all of us.

Sincerely Johan Bjorklund, in writing

Christmas Traditions

T raditions are wonderful. They define us as a family. They set goals for living for the younger generation. They establish who we are as a cultural group (such as Norwegian). They draw people together for happy celebrations. They create legends for storytelling, family history, and for remembering who are as a family.

Traditions are wonderful. The family-get-togethers help to strengthen and raise family members above insults or hurt feelings, real or imagined that always seem to be there. They create a sense of family that is ours alone.

As we drove to church Christmas Eve, we could hear the church bells chiming for the 5:00 p.m. service, just as the stars were coming out. The air was cold and crisp and clean. Walking in to worship together as a family was a dear family tradition. The singing of Christmas carols, the beautiful solos, the hymns of praise created a holy atmosphere. The joyous greetings of "Merry Christmas" to our friends and neighbors completed the perfect evening.

The drive to our house was well lit both inside and out. People's outer wraps were thrown on the bed and the women headed to the kitchen to help and to visit. The men and children gathered in the family room to wait for dinner.

There was no variation in the menu. Lutefisk was prepared, mashed potatoes were soon ready, along with meatballs and gravy. Drawn butter for the lefse, cranberry sauce, and coleslaw were placed on the table.

Adding to the festive décor were tall red candles and a centerpiece made of Swedish crystal with Mary and Joseph, and the Christ child, in the midst of angels and evergreens. The table felt like Christmas.

After dinner, the children were getting restless and tired. It was time to gather around the Christmas tree in the living room. First, the Christmas story from the Bible read by Dad, and then the presents were shared.

With oohs and aahs and childish delight, and hugs and thank yous for the gifts, it was all over too soon. It all happened too fast. Mom was especially grateful for the lutefisk turning out, along with the rest of the meal. Dad was happy that everyone else was happy.

Traditions are wonderful year after year.
Looked forward to dearly each time they come near.
But they do come faster the older we get.
Thank God for wonderful family traditions yet.

Rat-a-tat-tat

Rat-a-tat-tat, Rat-a-tat-tat, Rat-a-tat-tat. Uncle Gordon was watching, with a pleased gleam in his eye. It was Christmas Eve the year Arthur was seven. What a perfect gift for his nephew, Arthur, as he, Gordon, could go home at the end of the evening.

A loud noise continued from the toy submachine gun. I am sure it would be outlawed today. (Yesterday would have been soon enough, too.) It was horribly loud, so when it got to be too much for everyone to handle, we all joined in with, "SHUT IT OFF!" But how could Arthur do that when he was having so much fun? This quiet boy was having the time of his life. He was the center of attention in a family of four siblings. The end of the evening finally came with bedtime. I am sure one dear boy had his gun tucked near his side for the night.

Christmas Day arrived early, and between church and dinner, the Rat-a-tat-tat continued, much to everyone's annoyance. But, what do you suppose happened next?

Arthur was coming out of the bathroom, gun in hand, but there was an obstacle course in his way. He had to cross between the piano and the open hallway to the dining area and the edge of the wall that formed our living room. Being a novice at handling guns, and always in a hurry, he lifted the gun up horizontally in front of him. The barrel hit the side of the wall and broke in two. Gone were the Rat-a-tat-tats forever. Most of us were happy, but not one sad little boy.

(He also got a BB gun that year, so it made up the difference.)

Enjoying the Fireplace

When Donald and I were married, the shelter belt we planted around our dwelling was very short. We had good protection from the winds from the south and east, but not from the north and west. It was wide open country for miles. When the snow and proverbial winds would blow from the northwest, we had no protection other than to stay indoors. I remember several winter days when there was a complete whiteout. We could not see a thing outside our windows, except the blinding snow. The howling wind traveled for miles across the wide-open prairie. It slammed against our new house with much force. We thanked God for our Andersen Windows which were secure and tight. It took about ten years for our shelter belts to be tall enough for protection.

We had our fireplace built our first fall and it worked very well. I do not think Don's dad was too pleased about the fireplace idea. I am sure it was an extravagance in his mind. He said, "I've always heard that building a fireplace is a good way to cool off a house." It was true! The fireplace drew the house heat right up the chimney. Because of the heat of the fireplace, the furnace quit running, and the three bedrooms on the north got cold. In the early fall, a cozy fire took the chill out of the house. Oh! Could anything be nicer than a blazing fire to warm us up when coming in from outside?

Flat Broke

I t was time to get ready for church and Sunday school one Sunday morning. In the process of going out the door, I opened my billfold, looking for some small change. I had a few small bills but no small change at all. I told my young daughter to tell her teacher that Mom did not have any coins that day for Sunday school offering.

When my daughter arrived at Sunday school for opening exercises, she announced, "Momma was flat broke so she couldn't give any money." It was all the Sunday school superintendent could do to keep a straight face, but before church started, she came over and whispered in my ear what my daughter had said. We sat with silly grins on our faces well into the church service. Good thing the sermon came later in the hour.

Kindness Revisited

My first impressions of Karla were good when we met in the writing class. She seemed kind and compassionate, and personally interested in all our class members. I had lost my husband a few months earlier and my emotions were very close to the surface. She encouraged us to write each week at writing class.

The most amazing thing about Karla was that she noticed I did not physically write very well. The nerve endings in my right hand and fingers were damaged during surgery a few years before. As a result, writing was and is very difficult. She kindly called up a few days later and offered to type my stories into the computer, if I read them to her. What an expression of selfless love and kindness! She told me later that she felt sorry for me. Each week, Karla drove over some time before class to type and print out my stories for the assignments due that week.

It was fun! I enjoyed her so much. She never criticized my writing and continued to encourage me to write. By fall, I felt I was comfortable enough to ask her if she would read the stories I had written earlier, about 75% of the stories in my first book *Nurtured by Nature*. I offered to pay her, but she said, "No, I will be happy to read them." I was trembling in my boots as I asked her. After all, Karla Smart Morstad, Ph.D., was a professor for thirty years at Concordia College, Moorhead, Minnesota. Later, I had enough nerve to ask her if she thought it was worth the time and effort to pursue a book publication. She agreed. So, we continued on.

She and her husband, David Morstad, had computer expertise and knew all the details to prepare my manuscript for publication. Karla was always so kind to say, "It's all your writing, Alice, the stories are all yours."

We had a format to follow from WestBow Press. It is a Christian subsidiary of Thomas Nelson Brothers and Zondervan. They specified exactly how we were to put it all together. Then we had to proofread each story four times, making corrections as needed.

Finally, we received word that my manuscript was accepted for publication! We received two copies to proofread again and accept my book as they determined – the layout, the front cover, the back cover, and the jacket for the hardcover book.

I had no idea how long this process would take, but about four months later, we received word that the books were in print. The day finally came that the books arrived. We were all so pleased! We thought the publishers had done a beautiful job.

All this joy because Karla went the extra mile all the way through to publication, a perfect example of kindness made perfect. I feel so indebted to Karla and David Morstad. I would never have been able to accomplish all this without their expertise and help.

Thanks be to God who does all things well!

Four Lovely Ladies

T his how it happened.

Four lovely ladies, all blood sisters of about retirement age, came to Abercrombie, North Dakota, this fall to visit. Each year they planned a trip deciding together where to go. Two were from California, one from Florida, and one from Chicago, Illinois. This year they wanted to check out their roots. As they met my son, they told that they were descendants of Ingebricht Knute (I.K.) Gunness, a brother to Don's grandfather, Peter Knute (P.K.) Gunness. I. K. and P.K were the sons of Knute Gunness, the ancestor who came from Norway with his five family members.

The siblings told how their grandfather, Christian Gunness, the son of I. K. Gunness, attended North Dakota Agricultural College, the new Agricultural Land Grant College in Fargo, North Dakota. He earned a degree in agricultural engineering and stayed at the home of his professor, whose last name was Bolley, He eventually married a Bolley niece. Christian became a distinguished professor at Massachusetts Institute of Technology, Boston, Massachusetts, for many years.

So, these lovely ladies were granddaughters of Christian Gunness. My son thoroughly enjoyed visiting with them. They traveled to several cemeteries in the area looking for the name Gunness.

When the ladies heard that I had written a book, they wanted to meet me. I invited them to come to Riverview Place, where I live, the next day for lunch. But I ended up in the hospital instead! Undeterred, they came visit me there.

The Gunness ladies came smiling into my hospital room as we greeted each other, these relatives that I never knew existed until a few days before. To quote the local newspapers of yesteryear, "A delightful time was had by all." What fun we had talking about long ago days and recent times. I felt that I had known them all my life. It was a distinct privilege to meet these new (to me) family members.

Before they left they promised to return! I autographed a copy of my book for each of them-- *Nurtured by Nature* (WestBow Press). They called the next day, before leaving for Chicago, saying they would read my stories to each other as they traveled. I hope they enjoyed reading as much as I enjoyed writing.

Precious Memories

Precious memories were made when Grandpa Gunness built a pony cart for Donald's pony Flicka. It was in the middle 1930s. Don was about six years old. He had a great time driving his cart around town and even taking it out in the country for a family visit.

Once Don was asked if he would deliver a young lady, in his pony cart, to the park pavilion. It was her Bridal Shower day. Everyone did fine until they came to the pavilion. They forgot how slippery the floor had become. It was used for dances during the summer months. The pony and cart entered the pavilion, and chaos reigned. Flicka, with her dainty hooves, could only do a sliding and dancing jig as she tried to keep her balance. Her feet were splaying in all directions as she tried to keep upright. It was an unexpected grand entrance and exit from the bridal shower. Don's grandmother said it best in her Norwegian brogue, "OH NAY! STOCKER SLITEN, LITTLE FLICKA!"

Don, with his good memory of his grandfather's gift, decided to build a go-cart for his six-year-old son. He put it together – it did not cost much – mostly materials he had on the farm, but it worked. Dad and son took off for the first trial run with Dad driving. As Peter remembers it, the go-cart was going about thirty miles an hour! Back to the farm shop they flew to turn the motor down to a safer speed. We soon had a well-worn racetrack in the yard. V-ROOM, V-ROOM, V-ROOM!

The go-cart was the star of the show for Peter's seventh birthday party, with all his boy classmates invited. It continued to provide hours and years of fun until it was outgrown and parked in the trees. Years later, our nephew, Steve, asked if he could bring it home to his son. Later on, Steve's son also had the pleasure of driving the go-cart.

Homemade and handy, I suppose it is now parked in trees on another farm, waiting to be brought back to life yet again with the next generation. Let it be known, much fun was had by all, and many happy memories live on.

The Harvest Moon

H e was about twelve years old and from Chicago!

He shared with us that he lived with his parents, who both had full-time jobs. I think he was an only child. He said he would sleep most of the day, while his parents worked, and then he would be awake all night.

We met him at Bible Camp. There was an attraction between him and our family. He was a fun kid. So, he came home with us for a week, with parental permission of course. I think he was also a bit homesick. Ours was an entirely different way of life for him to see.

One evening, for a little surprise, I took him for a ride out of our driveway. As we turned east, the big beautiful full harvest moon was just rising over the trees along the Red River. We sat and watched, as the darkening dusk turned to night sky and the stars came out.

He gasped at what he saw, "I have never seen the full moon before or the stars in the night sky." Big inner-city Chicago night lights hid them from his view. The boy was awed by the beautiful night sky.

I hope he will never forget the full moon. I hope the memory of the glorious sky stays with him forever.

The Missing Ring

She was a lovely young lady, quiet, soft-spoken, kind, demure, but maybe a bit flaky. My kids met her at North Dakota State College of Science. They all liked her. She enjoyed hanging out with our kids at the house where they were staying, over winter, in Wahpeton, North Dakota. When spring came, the owners of the house returned home from wintering in Arizona. Then our kids moved home and drove back and forth to school.

A few days later, the lady of the house called, and asked what happened to the small glass bowl in the kitchen cupboard. Our kids did not know anything about it. Remembering what it looked like, they got a replacement at a store in town. It did not get broken, that they knew for sure, but what had happened to it was a mystery.

The next school year, Sonja transferred to Concordia College in Moorhead, Minnesota for her junior and senior years. She lived in a suite, with three other girls, in a dorm. Everyone got along fine together.

Sonja begged me, "Mom, can I wear the ring from Grandma for a while"? It was very hard on me, but I finally relented, with the promise from Sonja that it would never be taken off her finger – the surest way to lose a ring. She promised!

Everything was fine until it was time to lay on the grass for sunbathing. Of course, someone decided that the rings should go off their fingers so they would be sure to tan evenly! Off went Grandma's ring from Sonja's hand, left in the dish with the others and forgotten, until a few days later when she remembered the ring and went to put it on. But whoa! The ring was missing! Her suite mates were as shocked as she. Then Sonja remembered. The day they took in the sun was the same day her friend from North Dakota State College of Science visited. She remembered the glass bowl that had disappeared. So, the girls paid a visit and asked that she hand over the ring. She denied everything. It was time to call home and tell me the news. We called all the pawn shops in the Fargo-Moorhead area, but nothing turned up. We were at the end of our ropes. We prayed earnestly for the ring to be returned.

About three months later, I answered the phone. It was the same girl. She asked for Sonja. I said, "She has nothing to say to you until you return my ring." She said, "That's why I am calling. I want to return the ring." I was flabbergasted and overjoyed!

She came to our house and handed back the ring. Then she said to me, "I suppose you will hate me forever, now." I looked her in the eye and said, "No, dear, I will love you forever for returning my ring." I gave her a big hug. Now Grandma's ring will stay on my finger until I die.

Strange Sightings

The early morning drive to Colorado Springs meant a thousand miles were ahead of us. Sarah had just graduated from college, and we were driving to see our older daughter, Sarah's sister Sonja. Sarah grabbed a pillow as we went out the door at 4:00 a.m. She cuddled up in the back seat and was soon fast asleep. I headed straight south on I-29 to Watertown, South Dakota, then west the rest of the journey.

Driving south, suddenly the Northern Lights were upon me. They were everywhere, surrounding my car in the most overwhelming, unbelievable, continuous flashing lights. I was literally surrounded by brilliant flashing lights of all colors, as I continued driving in the early morning hours. It was beautiful, almost another worldly experience. I had seen Northern Lights in the far distant heavens but never anything like this. They continued for miles, until the morning light started to appear.

It was almost too strange a story to tell. Who would have believed it? Years later, a young lady from my little town told the same story. She was on the same road at the same time I had been. I tried to tell her that I had seen the same thing. She seemed not to believe me. What would I have been doing out that early in the morning? I sat and listened as she told her story. It was confirmation that I had seen what I had seen, and that was all that mattered.

A Pregnant Pause

I t was a typical after school stop at the local grocery store. For me, because I had not been out of the house earlier, I may have needed something for supper; for the kids, a little treat after school helped shorten the long afternoon.

As I was unloading my grocery cart of a few items, one of my older girls, about eight years old at the time, very enthusiastically announced a bit of news to the clerk: "Guess what, Beverly?

> The horse is going to have a colt,
> the cow is going to have a calf,
> the momma pig is going to have little pigs,
> the dog is going to have puppies,
> and the cat is going to have kittens, and…"

After a deep breath with a pregnant pause (forgive the pun) she very excitedly announced,

"Momma is going to have a baby!"

I thought Beverly was going to lose it entirely, as she hooted with laughter. I stood there in a stupor, thinking to myself, "Did she really say that"? We could not help but laugh. I am sure that within twenty-four hours the story of my fifth pregnancy and all the animals was the talk of the town.

Ah, small town living!

White Out

Don and I attended a National Beekeepers Meeting in January for a number of years. Arthur, living at home at the time, would care for the farm while we were gone.

A beautiful Sunday morning emerged. No wind and a brilliant sunrise made the fresh, new snow on the ground look lovely. Everything was a pristine white with the morning sun making sparkling stars in the snow.

After breakfast, Arthur drove his pickup into town for *The Fargo Forum* Sunday morning edition. It was just a mile into town, but as he started to go home a sudden, very strong wind came up. He said with all the new snow, it became a white out. He could not see anything. His pickup was enveloped in a blowing, blinding world of white. He could not see the road or the sides of the road. He inched along, worrying that he would drive in the ditch and not be found. It was before cell phones. What he had were his tracks from going into town, still showing faintly in the snow. He could barely see them over the hood of his pickup. He arrived safely home, but a bit jittery. He learned just how fast a North Dakota winter storm can come up.

Looking Out the Window

O
h, how I looked forward to spring when the apple trees began blooming. We planted apple trees a year after our wedding. Some thrived and some did not. Some were crab apples, and some were eating apples. A classic Haraldson was planted, and we enjoyed, every year both the blossoms and the fruit.

One year when our girls were attending North Dakota State College of Science, about twenty years after Don and I planted apple trees, they came home before Mother's Day with a beautiful double-bloomed ornamental apple tree. A blossom held another blossom inside the first one.

We hurried to plant it, and it thrived down the years, growing larger each year. It was a showpiece in lavender and pink, so loaded with blooms the branches were hidden. And the perfume! It was exotic!

The variety was soon off the market as nurseries called it "not thrifty." The trees seemed to die from winter weather exposure. Mine kept on blooming as it was sheltered by a windbreak from the south.

One spring an elderly gentleman visited us and exclaimed, "If that were my tree, I would sit all day and look at it."

Chapter Four

To Have and To Hold

The Mystery of the Watch Fob

I hold this treasure, an antique over a hundred years old, in my hands and lovingly place it on my neck. It was a gift given to my father in 1910 when he departed from Sweden to come to America. It was a gift from the girlfriend he left behind – never to see her again.

The gift was a beautiful watch fob for the gold pocket watch he wore with his three-piece suit. The suit had a button-vest with a pocket on each side. One side held the watch with a chain that traveled to the other pocket. On the chain was fastened a beautiful locket with *her* picture in it.

I am sure she was hoping to hear from him soon. Maybe her dream was to come to America after he earned his fortune in this rich new country.

The square locket of old gold held scroll designs embedded on the front side. There was a stone fastened with six tiny prongs as well. On the back were engraved the initials JB, for John Bjorklund, my father.

The mystery was hidden through the years. Who was she? Did she also come from the landed gentry (landowners)? How long had they been friends? It did not bother my Mother at all. The locket stayed in the jewelry box, long forgotten. Everything changed. No more three-piece suits. No more pocket watches as wrist watches came in style.

How serious was their relationship? Did she marry later, or did she die a lonely and perhaps bitter old woman? Had it been unrequited love?

Maybe we will never know the answer to this mystery.

I am glad my dad married my mother, in St. Paul, Minnesota, because otherwise I would not be here to tell this story.

I treasure the locket, and placed in it a picture of my granddaughter, Silje, rather than the "other woman." I value it as one of my favorite pieces of jewelry.

Love Story #1

My first love story is an ancestral story. This was long before my time on earth, so I am telling you the facts as I know them.

His name was KNUTE GUNNESS. He immigrated to America in 1882, coming to the Colfax-Abercrombie settlement of Norwegians, who also came from Rennebu, in the center of the country, about 200 miles north of Oslo. Knute was in his fifties and brought with him five children. He left behind the grave of his wife, nameless to me, who died in her fifties. It must have been terribly heart breaking to leave her grave behind and set out for the unknown. I remember seeing a picture of her and she was beautiful.

Knute was not a farmer by trade. He was a businessman, a blacksmith who repaired wagon wheels, rebuilt broken parts that he designed himself, and anything else that needed fixing. He soon established a thriving business, coming to Abercrombie in 1884 and setting up shop. He was successful and established himself in the pioneer town, where just twenty years earlier there had been a terrible Indian uprising from southern Minnesota to Fort Abercrombie. With military reinforcements, the fort was saved and all who were there for protection.

Knute, discovering how lonely he was without his wife, at one time sent a letter back to Norway to a lady he knew. She was a spinster, never married, and if a photograph can tell you something, she looked stern and hard. He arranged for her trip, and met the train north of Abercrombie, flagging down the train crew and bringing her the rest of the way home.

When the children were asked how it was with her, the only answer was, "It was better than no mother at all."

So begins the story of the Knute Gunness Family in America. Knute was my husband Donald Gunness' great-grandfather.

Love Story #2: Arthur and Adelia

It was in the early 1920s. They were born in the Centennial year 1900. Adelia, or Dilly as she was affectionately called, was born in Morris, Minnesota, the youngest of eleven children for Norwegian parents and landowners. Because her mother believed in education, Dilly attended St. Cloud Teachers College. After several years of teaching grade school in western Minnesota, she came to Abercrombie, North Dakota and was hired as a first and second grade teacher. One of the town's older gentlemen told me later that Adelia was one of the most beautiful ladies to come to Abercrombie.

Arthur Gunness, or Art as he was called, worked with his dad in the P.K. Gunness and Sons Blacksmith Shop. His was one of many businesses in the thriving pioneer town at the time. The town of Abercrombie was the second oldest town in the state, after Pembina, North Dakota, and established about twenty-five years earlier than others in the area. I came to Abercrombie as a new bride in 1956; the next spring, the community celebrated the town's centennial. Then the business was no longer a Blacksmith Shop, but the third generation Gunness Brother's Chevrolet Garage, with many other prosperous businesses in town.

As Art and Dilly discovered each other, they fell in love and were married in the 1920s. Art told about driving his model T along the trail next to the railroad track to Morris, Minnesota as there was no highway from Breckenridge, Minnesota at that time. By car today, it is about a two-hour drive; the 1920 route must have taken all day. The trip took Art to see his sweetheart, Dilly, during summer vacation from school. It must have been true love, but there is more to this story.

Art and Dilly prepared for their wedding, having ordered the flowers and mailed the invitations, the couple each needed a physical checkup from a doctor before they were married. It turned out, to everyone's shock, that Art was diagnosed with tuberculosis. It was a sad day when he came home from the doctor's office with the news. The family went into mourning, as TB was usually considered a death warrant. But Great-Grandmother Randine Gunness stated emphatically, "We're not going to give up yet!" Many prayers for returning health were sent to heaven for Art.

Dilly's older brother, a young medical doctor and surgeon, urged her, "dump him." Art's chances for survival were very slim. He entered a sanitarium somewhere in Minnesota. He was there two years, gradually improving until he was discharged and returned home. Their prayers had been heard and answered.

Art and Dilly were happily married for many years. Donald, their son and my husband, said he never remembers his dad as ever being sick a day in his life.

Love Story #3:
The Announcement

We had just left my parent's home before our wedding, just time to be together before our evening wedding ceremony, March 25,1956.

All of a sudden, my groom to be told me this: "I don't always feel good." I was dumbfounded. What did this mean? What is he trying to say to me? A quiet calm came over me and I remembered these words from a Shakespeare sonnet:

"Let us not to the marriage of true minds admit impediments;
Love does not alter when it alteration finds."

It was too late to ask questions, as we had just arrived at my sister's home next to the church where the family gathered.

My mind was going full speed. I knew this man was the kindest man I had ever known. I knew he was ambitious and hard working. I had never met anyone with whom I was more comfortable. And I knew he loved me and would always provide.

But me, I did not know the first thing about love, though I thought I did. I found out later that love is helping me in the middle of the night: "You take the bedding down to the laundry, and I'll clean up the baby and change his clothes." Love is taking over the family meal preparation while I was lying in bed sick. Love is acceptance and carrying on. His heart was always with the underdog and he helped as he could.

Yes, I knew in my heart I had made the right decision. I later found out what "I don't always feel good" meant. Sometimes in the middle of the morning, he would come into the house and lie down on the bed and close his eyes. After checking him over the doctor said Donald was having a migraine headache without the pain. Just flashing colored lights in his eyes, and a very scary sensation. He rested until feeling better and out the door he would go.

I realized many years later, after his diagnosis of a fast-growing brain tumor, in his late eighties, that maybe he had suffered for years, the result of being run over as a three-year-old by a car his dad drove. Don had been hiding in the rumble seat, got scared and jumped out the back. The wheel ran over him on his neck and shoulder. I wrote more completely about this story in my first book *Nurtured by Nature*.

I would not trade away any of it. We loved each other and were faithful to each other through sixty years of marriage. Suffering produces qualities in us that cannot be produced in any other way. Thanks be to God.

Love Story #4:
A Norwegian Wedding

W hat a way to go! Sarah made plans to come home early on Christmas Eve from Colorado Springs. She was to fly from Colorado Springs to Denver to Minneapolis to Fargo, but there were problems. She was bumped from the airlines at each airport. She kept calling us about the change in plans, and the calling kept on and on and on. It was better than waiting at the airport in Fargo. It was after 11:00 when she got home that night. She burst happily through the door and announced, "Mom, this year we are going to go to Norway and Sweden! I got a $1500 voucher for being bumped." So, we made plans to travel later in the year. I thought to myself, "We'd better go this year because next year she may be married."

In making travel arrangements, Sarah and I planned to fly to Stockholm and then drive to my father's farm in Kilafors, Sweden. We were invited to stay at my cousin's house. We then planned to rent a car and travel to my husband's family in Norway. In the process, we realized we did not know about driving in either country. So, Sarah asked in her church group if anyone knew anything about driving over there. One fellow spoke up and answered, "I know just who you should contact, and he will help you. He's from Norway, and he's not married either. I'll give you his phone number and he'll be happy to help."

She called and oh, what a nice sounding man. Soon they were going mountain biking and casually dating. She learned that he had a

Ph.D. in electrical engineering and was educated in Europe. Now he was designing computer chips for Maxim in Colorado Springs. Sarah made the statement that she surely hoped he would call her when we returned home. He did! Did I remember to tell you that they were both thirty-three years old and just about giving up finding the right one? He was just five days older than Sarah. They fell in love and he gave her a beautiful diamond ring at New Year's. They were married the next summer. Talk about our answer to many prayers.

⟵⟶

Sarah and Geir Ostrem were married in Moorhead, Minnesota, at the Hjemkomst Center in the Stave Church, with the reception following. In honor of Geir's nationality, it seemed only fitting. His parents flew in from Norway for the wedding. A Lutheran pastor, also of Norwegian descent, performed the ceremony in both Norwegian and English. Geir's mother did not speak English. It was lovely. July 20, 2002

Meeting Geir's parents, his mother expressed concern about her son marrying an American girl. I told her that she had nothing to worry about with Sarah, "She will make a wonderful wife for Geir."

Don and I thought very highly of Geir. After two children and sixteen years of marriage, Geir said to me, "Sarah is truly incredible." Her parents agree!

Chapter Five

Death Doesn't Become Her

The Day They Said I Died

I came down to the dining room for noon lunch, and the ladies at the table gasped as they saw me... "Alice, we heard you had passed away!"

They told me this story:

One of the older men, close to 100 years old, announced that he had seen my death notice in the Fargo morning paper! "Gunness from Abercrombie," he said. The ladies at the table questioned it. One lady said she had walked by my apartment and had not seen anything unusual. But, what can you see through a closed door? They thought I was in pretty good health at dinner the night before.

"Well, go down to the library and check it out. *The Fargo Forum* is sitting there." He then went to all five tables at breakfast telling them the news about me.

They did and found the death notice. Yes, it said the last name was Gunness, and the town was Abercrombie, but the first name did not match. The woman who died was my sister-in-law, Lois Gunness. Sadly, she died the previous Sunday.

In the meantime, news had spread like wildfire. When I came to the dining room for evening dinner, the ladies were all talking about me, too. They had heard the news that I had died. I laughingly told them, "I'm still here!" And that's how fast rumors fly.

I am surely glad that I am still here for another Riverview Writing Crew class.

The Day I Almost Died

I awoke at midnight for my nightly trip to the necessary room. When I returned to my bed, I was not breathing well. My diaphragm was heaving up and down as I tried to get my air. I was not having any chest pains but there was tightness.

I did not know what was wrong. I called the nurse on night duty and she came quickly. She took one look at me and said, "You need to go to the hospital. I'll call the ambulance." The ambulance crew arrived quickly and began the procedures needed to get me to the hospital. They put me in a wheelchair and out the door we went. In the ambulance, they put in an IV and placed a blood pressure monitor on me. We were on our way to the hospital.

I do not remember much after that except arriving and the tests taken. A cardiologist came. As I was being transferred to the operating room, the doctor said, "You are having a heart attack." When I came out of surgery several hours later, I was transferred back to the emergency room. Someone told me I had one stent put right in the middle of my heart and a balloon treatment on the other side.

I went home three days later and continued to improve. But while I was still in the hospital, I asked the doctor which artery was completely plugged. He said, "The Widow Maker." I was very thankful I survived.

The Day My Son Thought I Died

I was returning to my apartment from a meeting of the Riverview Writing Crew one Thursday afternoon. I was not feeling well, so I decided to call my son and have him take me to the emergency room. I met Mary Jo in the hall and she inquired about how I was feeling. She told me to come into her office so she could take my blood pressure as the nurses were busy. My blood pressure was low, so she suggested we call my son and tell him that I was in her office. She did not want me walking any further toward my apartment. She called him, introduced herself as Mary Jo, Spiritual Director, and told him to come to her office instead of to my apartment.

He immediately panicked as he drove to Riverview, drawing the conclusion that a Spiritual Director had to be someone who dealt with families who had lost loved ones. He thought I had died. It was with great relief that he saw me sitting in her chair. Mary Jo and I apologized for the scare. All's well that ends well!

Chapter Six

A Pot Pourri of Alice's Favorites

Just Pulled Over

It was my turn to be a jail visitor for the local Gideon Organization. I arrived at 9 a.m. with an hour to visit. I asked the jailer to come and get me at 10 a.m., as I was planning to go by my house to pick up my husband, and then attend church at 10:30. Loud clanging metal doors told me I was not going anywhere without the jailer.

The jailer was ten minutes late, so my time to go home was cut short. When halfway home, I saw the car coming around the only curve in the road ahead. Yikes! Highway Patrol! Coming from the opposite direction with lights flashing! I pulled over and the officer asked me for my driver's license. I explained that my purse was in the trunk of the car, and I needed to retrieve it.

After I pulled out my purse, I noticed the patrolman had retreated to his car to stand behind the open door. I suspected he had his hand on his gun, not knowing what to expect. As I was taking out my driver's license, I told him that I had just come from the jail. With a surprised look he asked, "What were you doing there?!"

I replied, "I've just come from visiting a lady in the jail as a Gideon Auxiliary member. I was on my way to pick up my husband to go to church, but the jailer was late in letting me out." I explained that I was speeding because I was going to be late. The reason my purse was in the trunk was because I could not bring it into the jail with me. I left my watch at home, too.

He checked over my driver's license, all was good. No ticket! We were on friendlier terms now. I told the officer that I would really have to speed now to get to church on time. He said with a thin smile on his face, "Well, please try to hold it down a little." I tried. But we still did not make it to the church on time.

An Apple Pie Demonstration

It all began with a branch my husband grafted to our apple tree from his mother's summer apple tree of many years. Beginning to ripen in the middle of August, they were delicious, sweet and tangy, good to eat out of hand and for baking. As they ripened, they were so juicy. The apples became translucent and made wonderfully flavored apple pie.

In my junior year of college, I took a class called Experimental Cookery. I concentrated on pie crusts. Each item was both weighed and measured then sampled at the end of the class period with evaluation by the class. My recipe for a single pie crust was: 1 cup flour, 1/3 cup cold lard, ½ teaspoon salt, and 4 tablespoons cold water. I had lots of experience over the years!

Moving ahead about twenty-five years, Don and I joined Toastmasters International, meeting in Wahpeton, North Dakota every week. One particular week my assignment was to give a demonstration speech. Since it was still summer apple season, I wondered if I could demonstrate making an apple pie.

At home I set to work. First, I made a complete pie, baked for serving at the meeting. I also prepared another filling of 6 cups of apples, thinly sliced, 1 cup sugar, 3 tablespoons instant tapioca, and 1 teaspoon cinnamon.

Then I gathered all the ingredients for the demonstration pie. First, the dry ingredients were placed in a mixing bowl, refrigerated cold lard was placed in a carrying box with the pie plate, rolling pin, and a pastry cloth for rolling. I had cold water measured out, flour for rolling the pie crust, and a wet cloth for wipes.

That evening, I set up the demonstration before the meeting. I told the emcee for the evening, "I am putting on a TV cooking program," so that he would properly introduce me when I came onto the stage. With the audience applause, I entered and began my demonstration.

I talked as I worked the lard by hand into the flour mixture, adding the water after the lard was mixed. I had to work fast as it was only a half hour program. After shaping the two balls of dough, I began to roll out the crust, turning it over several times to make sure it was evenly rolled. I folded the thin dough in half and put it into the pie plate. I rolled out the second crust which I then set aside.

The apple mixture came next, pouring into the bottom crust with a pat of butter in the middle for flavor. Then the top crust went on. I showed how to trim and fold the edges, to crimp with my thumb and two fingers, to make a nice edging to keep the juice inside. A little milk was smoothed on by hand with a sprinkle of sugar on top and a few slits to let the steam escape.

There it was: a completed apple pie!

At the close of the meeting, we all shared a small piece of apple pie, and everyone agreed. "Alice knows how to make a good pie!" In the allotted time period, too!

Collecting

At my age, I am tired of collecting earthly treasures. When I was younger, I was so proud of my possessions—Swedish crystal vases and decorative dishes, deep red bud vases, with sugar and creamers to match. When we went to Fergus Falls, Minnesota, I would stop at the Norwegian Shop or in Fargo, North Dakota, at the Stabo shop. Items were imported and beautiful with a price tag to match. When my dear friend from younger years sold her home and moved, of all that was left, she gave me a set of twelve goblets and matching sherbets which were wedding gifts from her husband's aunt (circa 1910-1920). Twenty years ago, they were worth about $20 a goblet. What are they worth today? I used them with affection for holidays and special occasions. But now they sit in my breakfront, tipped upside down, peeking through the glass doors, waiting to be needed.

Modern conveniences have taken over, and when family members come, always in a hurry, there is no time for extra touches – the gracious living of yesteryear. Grilled hamburgers, with onions, potato salad, and baked beans are served. Maybe someone will bring a pie. Paper plates and cups are used with hardly anything to fill the dishwasher anymore. But we have survived and now I want to collect hugs and kisses from my family and grandchildren. That is the best collection.

Surprise!

It was a long five-hour ride to our daughter's house that early April. This was a special occasion as the second baby was to be baptized that day.

The landscape was dreary all the way. Spring was fighting with winter. Who was in control? The sun that morning was mostly on our back as we traveled west. For the last hour of our journey, after turning south, the bright sun hung low in the sky. We had full benefit of its warmth in the car. I had put on perfume before I left home because I knew there would be hugs, and grandmas must smell good. But after five hours, could there be any perfume left? I was getting warm and a little sweaty besides.

When we arrived, the rest of the family were all gathered in the big kitchen area, awaiting us. My son-in-law's family was all there, including aunts and uncles and cousins and elderly family members, too.

We walked in to everyone's greetings. Grandpa, my husband Don, asked for a big hug from our grandson who was four years old at the time. Don then said, "Give Grandma a big hug, too!" I sat down on a chair, and he came over and gave me a hug. But then he pulled back and looked at me and said, "Grandma you smell …" There was a long pause with everyone holding their breath not knowing what to expect and fearing the worst. I glanced up at the audience and saw a sea of worried faces. What was he going to say? He blurted out the word, "… beautiful!" A sigh of relief was heard by all. There were smiles and people clapped for such a good answer. I was sure his parents were most proud. I gave him another big hug. I thought of this Bible verse, "Out of the mouths of babes and children come perfect praise."

What Mothers Do

It was daughter's last test of spring quarter at North Dakota State College of Science. School was over for the summer. Her final test was finished by 1:30 p.m., and she really wanted to come home. But there was a problem. Her sister Sonja was working at a lady's dress shop until 5:30 p.m. that day. On that lovely spring day, she wanted to come home and ride her horse. I well understood her feeling. "I just need to get out of here," she said.

But there was another problem. I had mixed up and kneaded a big batch of whole wheat bread dough starting with four cups of water. It made five loaves which fit into my oven perfectly. Well, what could I do? It was not ready to be placed in pans for baking, but she wanted me to come and pick her up, just twenty miles away.

A thought came to me that I could bring my big round stainless-steel bowl with me. The weather conditions were perfect for the bread dough to rise. It was warm and the humidity was high, and it was just the right temperature for the yeast to grow. I knew if the dough rose too high, we would have coarse grained bread. It would not be right.

So, into the car with me went my bread dough, with a kitchen towel over it, keeping me company in the front seat. I punched the bread dough down once and turned it over, and I was on the road again. It was rising so quickly, that by the time I picked up my girl, I had to punch it down again. Of course, we had a few little errands to run, so more delays. I punched down the dough again! By the time we returned home, the bread dough had been punched five times. I quickly shaped my loaves to rise again before putting them in the oven. The taste and texture of the bread was so fine and good, the family all bragged about my bread turning out so well. We all laughed at dinner about how it had been accomplished. As I have heard over the years, "Where there is a will, there is a way!"

That Glorious Day

F riday, July 13, 2018, was the day chosen for my book signing at Riverview Place, in Fargo, North Dakota. Karla Smart-Morstad, my mentor and friend, and I were interviewed earlier in the week by Tracy Briggs of *The Fargo Forum*, regarding my experiences writing *Nurtured by Nature*. *Forum* photographer Dave Samson accompanied her. We were pleased with the interview. Tracy said, before leaving, that her story had to be approved before printing. I gave her a copy of my book.

WestBow Press promised that the books would arrive in time for the Friday event. We waited in anxious anticipation for them to come, all 150 copies. Could you have a book signing without books? Finally, at 7:00 p.m. on Wednesday evening, there was a knock on the door. The books had arrived.

My daughter, Sarah, and family – husband Geir, Silje, 15, and Trond, 11 – arrived from Colorado Springs, Colorado the day before the signing. Our two sons, Arthur from Abercrombie, North Dakota and Peter from Minneapolis, Minnesota were there. Our daughter, Mary, arrived from western North Dakota. We were all watching *The Fargo Forum* for the anticipated article. Nothing on Tuesday, nothing on Wednesday, nothing on Thursday. By Friday, I was afraid to look. That morning Sarah picked up a paper to find a story in the Life Section with a big headline "A Dream Decades in the Making." Silje read the story aloud in the car as they made their way from the hotel to Riverview that morning. They were so excited about the beautifully written story. What a wonderful way to start the day.

Sister Faith Wanner and Kelly Brekke, Activities Directors at Riverview Place, made all the arrangements before the party. From public event invitations to table decorations, then serving coffee and cupcakes, they were in charge. Two dozen roses decorated my book signing table. Excitement was in the air. At age eighty-five, I was the first published author at Riverview Place. After reading the feature story in *The Forum,* and going to the book signing, some wag made the statement, "The crowd is bigger than for a funeral."

Polly, from our business at home, was the cashier for the day, writing the names of all who purchased books. The crowd kept coming until it was standing room only! Family and friends from home, and strangers from the community, arrived with those from Riverview. Writers from Riverview Writing Crew were there to support me. What a special day.

At the beginning of the program, Karla introduced me to the audience. I read several short stories from my book which everyone seemed to enjoy. The following days I had many compliments about how people identified with my stories. They said they could not stop reading once they started.

What a glorious day! I give the glory to Jesus for providing such an experience, one I never dreamed possible.

Chapter Seven

Inspiration

My Heroes of the Day!

A sudden summer afternoon thunderstorm blew-up near Walcott, North Dakota, about twenty miles from Abercrombie, North Dakota.

A sudden lightning strike hit the white, wooden church steeple and bell tower of Walcott Lutheran Church. A fire and flames erupted. The steeple stood out tall and beautiful above the treetops. Fire departments were called from neighboring towns. All were volunteers which slowed their coming. Firefighting equipment was limited and poor. Fires were dreaded. Every community had gone through them, sometimes losing whole blocks of businesses.

My husband Donald, a teenager at the time, just happened to be in the Gunness Brothers' Garage, owned by Don's dad and uncle. The phone rang, an urgent call from Walcott, explaining the water hoses were too short to reach the fire in the church steeple. "C'mon, Donnie, let's go! Hurry up," Uncle John ordered. "Help me hook up the chemical firefighting trailer to the pickup." Don did and jumped in the vehicle. They took off at record speed.

Remember, the county roads in the 1940s were still gravel. (For example, US County 81, which went all the way to Mexico, was not tarred until the 1950s.) When Don and his uncle arrived, everyone was very relieved. Don and Uncle John unhooked the trailer and proceeded to lug the equipment up to the attic of the church. They were able to spray retardant into the bell tower and put the fire out.

They were heroes of the day! They saved the church from burning. For several years after we were married, we drove to Walcott for the Annual Walcott Lutheran Church Lutefisk Dinner.

The church still stands. Don and Uncle John were heroes; the story has long been forgotten by others. But I know, and now you know, and his grandchildren will know, too.

With Grateful Hearts

A thankful spirit, a spirit of gratitude, needs to be cultivated in our hearts as we look to God our Father to answer our prayers. It is written in His words, "God inhabits the praises of His people." (Psalms 22:3, NKJV)

In the same way that we expect to receive thanks for gifts given, God also expects us to thank and praise Him for all His gifts and blessings which are without number.

Let us continue to give our Father in heaven thanks and praise for all the gifts we receive from Him:

"For health and strength and daily food, we praise your name, oh Lord." (Bert Frederick Polman, 1945 – 2013)

Thanks for glorious sunrises and sunsets,
For waving fields of grain, like waves on the water,
For rustling corn as it ripens in the wind,
For the smell of the good earth after it rains,
For glorious full moons each month and the sun that comes each morning,
For family love that brightens each day,
For a baby's first smiles and happy giggles.

"Every good and perfect gift comes down from the Father of Lights," (James 1:17, NKJV) so let us be quick to offer thanks and praise in our hearts every day, not only on Thanksgiving Day.

Tributes

"A merry heart doeth good like a medicine."
Proverbs 17:22, NKJV

S ister Faith, you exemplify this scripture verse in your loving personality. You always share your happy smiles with everyone. You are always busy, whether helping others or always doing something extra.

Your personal touches were seen all over Riverview Place, in the bulletin boards, announcements, and your decorating touches in the hallways. Among all the things you did, you were in charge of the movies each week, calling bingo, leading exercise classes, supporting writers, and stepping in wherever needed with a happy and cheerful spirit.

"Thank you, Sister Faith," residents say, for your loving kindnesses. You live by your name, Sister Faith, every day.

Sister LaVonne, gracious and kind, you have kept the dining room humming every day. Whether it was early morning or noon, your eagle-eye assessed everything needed. You are a take charge woman! In bringing table orders, or a glass of water, or a pot of coffee, you were always ahead of us all, knowing just what we needed. You worked every day as a servant among us, knowing that, as Jesus said, "If you want to be great you must be a servant of all." (Matthew 20:26)

You are gratefully thanked for your loving spirit every day.

Sister Faith and Sister LaVonne, you have been the heart and soul of Riverview Place. Your loving ways reflect our Lord's life as you continually give to others.

My God bless you every day as a reward for serving others.

Happy Easter

A s I was surfing through the TV programs one day, there was a world-known evangelistic service showing thousands of black people in the heart of Africa. They were standing and worshiping God with hands raised high. The joy of the Lord was on their lips. They had received their Savior and Lord, and the assurance of their salvation and life eternal. I marveled. It seemed so easy for them to ask Jesus into their hearts. It seemed as though every hand was raised at the huge outdoor assembly of people.

Then the thought came to me that these hordes of people had nothing to lose and everything to gain. They had experienced terrible sufferings and had known fear and despair in their lives. Now, they had received the gift of hope and love, both for this life and the life to come. They were rejoicing. It was real.

When Jesus walked on the earth, He talked about who would inherit eternal life. He said, "Narrow is the way and few there be who find it." (Matthew 7:14, NKJV) "It is easier for a camel to pass through the eye of a needle than for a rich man to enter the kingdom of heaven." (Matthew 19:24, NKJV) These are strong words.

You are probably saying right now, "Well, that surely doesn't include me because I am not rich." Do you know that most of the world considers Americans to be rich in comparison with what they have? The Bible goes on to say, "Where your treasure is, there will your heart be also." (Matthew 6:21, NKJV)

At our age, the hard decisions are concerns: what to keep, what to give away, and what to throw away. When Jesus took our place at Calvary, He took it all, our sins, our sicknesses, and opened the door to eternal life. But He demands no less from us also. We must surrender our lives to Him and give Him our all. Which of our earthly treasures, faux gold, are we willing to surrender?

St. Paul the Apostle stated that he counted all his previous life as refuse or dung in comparison to the overwhelming worth of knowing Jesus Christ as Savior and Lord.

In the light of Eternity, is it too much to ask?

"Up from the grave He arose with a mighty triumph o'er His foes!"

(Robert Lowry, 1826-1899)

Because He lives, we too shall live.

HAPPY EASTER!

Time

Tell me, why is it? When you are in the biggest hurry, time races ahead of you.

When you are waiting for someone or something, how can time go so slowly? It is like the proverbial watched pot that never boils.

Why is it, when you are in the supermarket, and you are racing for time, there are not enough checkers? You wait and wait. Does time really go any slower?

When you say you will meet someone at such and such a time, a dozen interruptions take place. When you are patiently waiting in the doctor's office, the time is longer and slower than scheduled.

Why does time do this to us? An old saying is. "Time waits for no man," but we wait plenty of times for him. It is a matter of hurrying to wait, or sometimes we think we have plenty of time, but the stoplights slow us down and the road construction causes detours.

It is true each one of us is given twenty-four hours a day. But some people are habitually late and others extra early. An old gent from our town said, "It is better to be an hour early than a minute late." That does not always work either. Have you ever had company arrive a half-hour early while you are still in your scrubs? Or have you arrived at some gathering a day early or at the wrong time? Time plays tricks on us.

And how about the thought that each year the time goes faster. Did not your year go faster this year than last? When Riverview residents go down to dinner, we may be asked, "What did you do today"? First comes the pause, and then the answer, "Not much. I didn't have time to get anything done."

How are we going to understand it? It seems to be that for each of us, the twenty-four hours are different. Isn't it a miracle that we are ever able to come together at scheduled times?

Perspectives

" At different ages, you think differently," my husband's father often stated. What is my perspective at age eighty-five compared to twenty-five years ago? How do I perceive my family now? How have we grown? How do we consider life now as compared to earlier years?

Are "things" still as important as they once were? Or have our values changed? What do we now consider important? How have our hopes and dreams changed? Or are they still the same?

As we age, we have time to ponder and consider life from a different perspective. We have more time to meditate and pray. Looking back, we realize our mistakes, seek forgiveness, and then our hearts are cleansed from all unrighteousness.

What are the reasons for our hope? Or have we given up because there are no answers? Has life dealt us so great a blow that we never recover?

I do not know what all your answers are, but I do know that we are all different and unique, each in our own ways. We have a heavenly Father who cares and knows us, as He made us the way we are. He loves each of us as individuals and wants to develop a loving relationship with us, so that we may mature and grow and become the people God has called us to be.

Perspectives on the Pandemic

What is happening in our world today? Is God bringing judgment on us? Is His anger being poured out on the whole world? On the contrary, let us look at this pandemic explosion we are all going through as God's loving kindness and tender mercies to people all over the world. Maybe God in His mercies is giving us a much-needed wake-up call to return to Him.

We ask the question, "Why do we need God"? So many of us have everything we need, sufficient food; fancy homes loaded with *things*; beautiful cars; perfect two-children families—do I need to say more? Of course, we do not need God.

Yes, we do! Built into every person is a need for God. We must all face these words, "first comes death and then comes judgment." (Hebrews 9:27, NKJV) But God in His abundant mercies is not willing that any should perish. All should come to the knowledge of the Truth. This is our wake-up call because, yes, Jesus is coming back as His word declares. Maybe much sooner than it has ever entered our minds.

It is my personal belief that we should turn to God and ask forgiveness for thinking we do not need Him. We should turn in repentance to receive restoration. May we return God to His rightful place in our lives and receive new life in Christ. Whether we live or die, we are the Lord's and have passed from death into life through Christ. We are the Lord's!

Glorious Freedoms

An old pastor of thirty-four years in my church made this statement, "There is no sermon as powerful as the sermon of death." By contrast, I want to deal with the "Glorious Freedoms of the children of God." These glorious freedoms are many and they are ours. They all have to do with eliminating fears from our lives. The Bible says many times, "Fear not, do not be afraid." (Deuteronomy 31:6, NKJV) Christ has given us power to become overcomers in the world we live in.

He is able to free us from:

1. Fear of death and dying
2. Fear of the unknown, future
3. Fear of failing
4. Fear of the devil, the world, and our flesh
5. The power of sin to control our lives

Yes, these are the glorious freedoms that come from God the Father, through the shed blood of Jesus Christ. They are freely given to us as believers. There is a price, but it is worth it. Jesus gave His all on Calvary's Cross; He paid the price of sin and separation from God for the whole world, by His death. Our gift back to Him is our letting go and surrendering ourselves to God – everything, body, soul, and spirit.

Oh, how hard it is to do this. We cannot do it on our own; but He helps us with His Holy Spirit power. This is what Jesus calls "being born again," in the book of John.

As the Bible says:

"Oh death, where is thy sting? Oh grave, where is thy victory?" (I Corinthians 15:55, NKJV)

"But thanks be to God who gives us the victory through Jesus Christ our Lord." (I Corinthians 15:57, NKJV)

Gratitude – A Life Alphabet

I am grateful for:

Amazing Grace
Beautiful Savior
Christ my King
Devotion
Everlasting Life
Finished Redemption
God is my Father
Heaven is my home
Immortal, **I**nvisible, God Only Wise
Just as if I'd Never Sinned
Knowing Him as Savior and Lord
Loving Compassion
Mercies Unending
New Heavens and a New Earth
The **O**pen Tomb
Partners in Fellowship
Quiet and Rest
Radiance Divine
Salvation in No Other
Teaching Me
Unimaginable Love
Victories in Jesus
Worship in the Beauty of Holiness

eXtraordinary Salvation
Yieldedness
Zeal for Christ

"Every good and perfect gift comes down from the Father of Lights." (James 1:17, NKJV)

For all these things, I am grateful.

Our Presentation Sisters

The first year I moved to Riverview, I was often asked, "Were you here when the three Catholic sisters were in charge?" "No," I would reply. The residents then began to tell me how wonderful and capable they were. My curiosity continued. Who were these Irish Catholic Sisters that everyone loved so much? I saw the works of their hands all around me, the Chapel, the beautiful swimming pool, the decorative touches in the dining room, with cloth tablecloths and napkins, and seasonal centerpieces. I saw the lovely prints on the walls and the beautiful furniture in the public areas. All was well done. I was duly impressed.

Then I started to notice the friendly spirit among the residents, the employees, and the administration. Everyone is your friend. Church services are provided for all. We sense that we are surrounded by prayer. The Catholic Sisters still pray for us even though they are not here.

So, I want to pay tribute to and honor these Catholic Sisters who worked hard and played an important role in the residents' lives. They left a standard of excellence that now continues after they retired.

Sister Josephine was in charge of the dining room, food service, and workers. She taught the student workers how to set a table, how to dress, and how to serve correctly. Excellence is your name, Sister Josephine Brennan.

Sister Mary Beauclair was in charge of the physical grounds surrounding all five buildings. We are all recipients of the beautiful tree plantings and flower beds on the property. The perennial beds and the additional potted plants cheer our hearts. We see the evidence of all her work and efforts on our behalf in the beautiful mature trees.

Sister Agatha Lucy was on duty twenty-four hours every day and every night as a nurse. She told how in the early days, if someone needed help, she would take the residents to the hospital emergency room, adding spiritual help and waiting to bring them back home. She was on duty every day carrying on with her warm personality and spreading cheer wherever she went.

They all did whatever needed to be done, from reaching down to pick up a scrap of paper, to cleaning the restrooms at 10:00 at night. Their love and loyalty shown through their daily living, and they were much loved and respected by all.

So we pay honor and tribute to these capable women. They first gave themselves to Christ, then gave themselves to us in loving service.

To God be the glory for lives well-lived.

Wonderful

I suppose he was in his sixties when we first met him. We purchased some farmland near his in Minnesota. We were there that day checking things over, when an older Cadillac drove up to the field approach. He opened the door and extended his hand in greeting. With a Norwegian accent he said, "I'm Marvin Berg and I live down the road where the white house is standing. I hear you are buying this property. Wonderful! If you have need of anything, please stop by." He invited us in for coffee anytime. I think he was a bachelor brother, newly retired.

Jovial, good-natured, with his nicely rounded body always clad in overalls, he helped us to feel welcome. His speech was often interjected with the word, spoken very energetically, "Wonderful!"

One time when we did stop by his house, his kitchen sink was full of electrical tools and hammer and nails, along with pieces of roast chicken on the other side. We just drank coffee.

That word "Wonderful" rubbed off on all of us; Don started using the word often. It just made us feel good to say it. And now I hear Arthur, my son, saying it often.

Several years later we saw his obituary in *The Fargo Forum*. We went to his funeral in a white rural church with a beautiful steeple reaching toward heaven. After the service, we introduced ourselves to his older sister. Unlike her brother, she was dour faced, tall, thin, and stern. Don talked about Marvin and his "Wonderful" words. She replied with a condescending air, and disgust, "Oh, yes. He used that word all the time!"

She did not seem to realize that the name "Wonderful" is used in the Bible as one of the words for God. "Wonderful, Counselor, Mighty God, Everlasting Father, Prince of Peace" (Isaiah 9:6–7, NKJV) No wonder we felt good when we used that Word.

God's Love Songs

The glorious hymns of the church carry us through the long days and, sometimes, sleepless nights of our lives. As we grow older, they minister to us in timely ways.

"The love of God, how rich and pure
How measureless and strong,
It shall forever more endure.
The saints and angel's song."
(Frederick M. Lehman 1868 – 1953)

"Oh, isn't the love of Jesus something wonderful
Wonderful it is to me."
(John W. Peterson, 1921 – 2006)

"The old rugged cross made a difference...
So, I'll cherish the old rugged cross
And exchange it someday for a crown."
(George Bennard, 1873 – 1958)

"Nearer my God to Thee, nearer to Thee,
Even though it be a cross that leadeth me.
Still all my songs shall be
Nearer my God to Thee, nearer to Thee."
(Sarah Flower Adams, 1805 – 1848)

"I will sing of my Redeemer
And his wonderous love to me.
On the cruel cross he suffered
Paid the debt and set me free."
(P. P. Bliss, 1838 – 1876)

The poets of old said it better than I ever could. These hymns of faith have survived the centuries.

Many Names of Our Triune God

A. Almighty God; Alpha and Omega
B. Blessed Redeemer
C. Counselor; Creator
D. Divine God
E. Everlasting Father
F. G. Father God; God our Father
H. Holy Father; Holy Spirit; Holy One of Israel
I. Immortal God; Invisible; "I am who I am"
J. Jesus
K. King of Kings
L. Lord of Lords
M. Mighty God; Merciful Father
N. Now and forever, Amen; Name above every name
O. One God, world without end
P. Prince of Peace
Q. Quintessential Being
R. Righteous Father; Redeemer
S. Savior and Lord
T. Triune God
U. Unity of the Spirit
V. Victorious Jesus
W. Wonderful Counselor, Word of God
X. How eXcellent is Your Name
Y. Yeshua, (Hebrew Name for Jesus)
Z. Zion, City of our God

A Love Letter to My Family Members

I am sending each of you a Love Letter for Valentine's Day.

LOVE   I send you my love because love covers a multitude of sins. I cherish each one of you as my own precious child.

ACCEPTANCE   I send my gift of acceptance to each of you with all your individual gifts and blessings and personalities.

UNDERSTANDING   I send you the gift of understanding with all your individual talents and abilities and thank God for them all.

GOODNESS   I give you the gift of goodness because God has poured into our hearts His goodness and mercy, which are new every morning.

MERCY   I give you the gift of mercy so that the God we serve may continue to show mercy to us, as we may show mercy to others.

PEACE   I send you the gift of peace that it may be shed abroad in our hearts by the Holy Spirit, that others may also see peace in our lives.

JOY   I send you the gift of joy in your hearts because the joy of the Lord is our strength, and I want it for all of you.

FORGIVENESS   I give you the gift of forgiveness, for as we forgive others, God forgives us. Harboring unforgiveness in your heart against any leads to bitterness which defiles many.

FAITH   I give you the gift of faith for with faith one can move mountains of clutter of which we need to let go.

KINDNESS   I give you the gift of kindness. Be kind to one another and forget the faults of others, knowing that we have the same frailties.

PATIENCE   I send you the gift of patience, because as we show patience to one another, we share each other's burdens and so fulfill the law of Christ.

GENTLENESS   I send you the gift of gentleness. Be gentle in all your doings with others, because only God knows the hurts and bleeding hearts of others.

Please accept my gifts for Valentine's Day and always. As you receive these gifts and share them with others it becomes a double blessing in your lives.

The Gift of Suffering

It all began with my first knee surgery. When I was strapped to the operating table, someone did not put enough padding under my right elbow. As a result, I had nerve damage to my right hand. I woke up after surgery and found that my hand was numb, but nothing was done. As a result, I lost 80% of the use of my right hand from nerve damage. It was hard to bear, because I have been a doer all my life. Now I could not even carry a pan of potatoes from the sink to the stove, but my knee healed fine.

After much pain, a couple years later I needed my left knee replaced. After surgery, my left knee and leg swelled up like a football and was just as hard. The incision tore open. I had an open wound three inches long and two inches wide over my knee. It was filled with blood and fluid. The doctor later asked me, "When did this happen?"

"When I was still in the hospital," I replied. In the transitional care unit, I developed a blood clot in my left leg. Somehow the medical staff did not believe me. For nine days I walked and hurt as the blood clot moved up into my thigh. I called my daughter in Colorado Springs, Colorado, and she talked to the charge nurse. I guess she read them the riot act. They finally moved on it and I was transferred to Fargo, North Dakota, to an Intensive Care Unit. Yes, it was a blood clot after all.

I was then moved to a nursing home in Fargo for three weeks. The charge nurse was sharp and she told me I should go to the wound clinic downtown. Later at home, twice daily we cleansed and dressed my knee. For six months we drove to the wound clinic each week until it finally healed.

My knee has not returned to normal size as I still have some swelling. With my right hand and left knee, I became handicapped. I now use a walker to get around. It is hard to hold a pen to write.

A year and some months later in the fall, my husband, Don, was diagnosed with a fast-growing cancerous tumor in the brain. Then, at the worst time, I fell and broke my right arm above the elbow. I needed more care, as did my husband. I told the doctor, "You can't separate us now after sixty years of marriage."

We moved to Rosewood on Broadway, a most wonderful nursing home, in Fargo, North Dakota. We were only two doors from each other. The aides dressed me each morning and I could spend the day with Don. We had two wonderful, loving months together.

I later moved to Riverview Place, an assisted living facility. I am happy here and enjoy the staff, good food, and friendly people in a Christian atmosphere. A writing group started just after I arrived. Riverview Writing Crew has been a wonderful fulfillment of my dreams to continue writing. Karla and David, her husband, with all their computer expertise, helped me to have my first book, *Nurtured by Nature*, published.

If I had not broken my arm, I would not have been able to stay with my husband his last two months. If I had not been classified handicapped, and of need of an assisted living facility, I would never had found this wonderful place. I would never have found Karla and the writing group and classes. "God works in mysterious ways, His wonders to perform."

Lest We Forget

The *Faith* of our ancestors brought them across the mighty Atlantic and helped them say goodbye to family and loved ones. Our ancestors were looking for a better life.

The *Courage* that was theirs to conquer the difficult ocean voyage. (My mother said it was too horrible to talk about.)

The *Strengths* that enabled them to cross half the country to settle in North Dakota and Minnesota. They did not give up. They kept hanging on.

The *Endurance* to live in simple, crude claim shacks and sod houses until they were able to improve their lot.

They did it all for us. We inherit the beautiful farms and lovely homes they built. They wanted to make life better for us.

Let us remember they held on to their dreams for a better life for all, but they brought their sacred beliefs and lived them for us. They built schools, churches, farms and businesses, and communities all for our benefit.

As God is our Helper, let us continue to build on their foundations of *faith, hope, trust,* and *love* for our future generations as well.

Acknowledgements

A special thank you to Terry Sinner for volunteering her time, typing, and computer skills. She spent countless hours putting my handwritten stories and essays into electronic documents in preparation for my second book.

Thanks to Karla Smart-Morstad, and her husband David Morstad, for helping me continue writing my stories and for making my second dream a reality. Karla guided my writing. During the pandemic, when we could not be together, she took dictation over the phone so my writings could be typed for this book. She and David asked me questions to help me edit my writing. With his computer expertise, David formatted my manuscript and photos for publication.

Thank you to my son, Arthur Gunness, and my daughter, Sarah Ostrem, for their support and encouragement. They were always willing to listen to my stories.

Thank you to the members of the Riverview Writing Crew, led by Karla, David, and Rita Greff, for listening to my stories as they were read each week. Several originate from the writing prompts they provided.

Thank you to my granddaughter, Silje Ostrem, for suggesting the title for my first book. It was so fitting I used it a second time for *Nurtured by Nature: Book II.*

Thank you to my cousin, Håkan Persson, in Storvik, Sweden. He translated my parents' letters, written home to Sweden in the 1930s, back into English. He sent the copies that appear here. I am grateful for his interest in remembering the generations.

To Riverview Place, thank you for hosting our writing group and being a wonderful place to live.

Thanks to Dave Samson, photographer, and *The Fargo Forum* for permission to include a photo he took when I celebrated publication of my first book.

Thanks to Tracy Briggs for her wonderful news story about *Nurtured by Nature, Book I* in *The Fargo Forum*.

Thank you WestBow Press, my publishers, who gave invaluable help along the way to my second book.

Thanks to all who read my first book and encouraged me to keep writing.

My deepest thanks to my husband, Donald, who encouraged me and supported me in my early days of writing. Donald told me to always put a punch line at the end, and I have.

Praise to the Lord and Savior Jesus Christ, who has opened wonderful doors for me, including my friendships with Karla, David, and Terry for their writing expertise.